T
of
Joy

*To Willem
Love + Blessings,
Joy*

by Joy Jones

© 2016 Joy Jones
All Rights Reserved

The moral right of Joy Jones to be identified as the author of this work has been asserted in accordance with the Copyright, Designs & Patents Act 1988

All rights reserved. This book is copyright material and must not be copied, reproduced, transferred, distributed, leased, licensed or publicly performed or used in any way except as specifically permitted in writing by the author, as allowed under terms and conditions under which it was purchased or as strictly permitted by applicable copyright law. Any unauthorised distribution or use of this text maybe a direct infringement of the author's rights and those responsible maybe liable in law accordingly.

Scripture quotations taken from the The Holy Bible, New International Version (Anglicised edition) Copyright © 1979, 1984, by International Bible Society. Used by permission of Hodder & Stoughton Publishers, an Hachette UK company. All rights reserved. "NIV" is a registered trademark of International Bible Society. UK Trademark Number 1448790

Scripture taken from THE MESSAGE. Copyright © 1993, 1994, 1995, 1996, 2000, 2001, 2002. Used by permission of NavPress Publishing Group.

Contents

Dedication	5
Acknowledgements	6
Endorsements	8
Foreword	12
Introduction	13
1. The Birth of Joy	15
2. Learning about Jesus	25
3. Getting to know Jesus	33
4. The Years of Change	41
5. Lost at Sea	49
6. Outpouring of God's Kindness	59
7. Saved by Grace	69
8. Repent and be Baptised	81
9. A New Creation	89
10. Food Provided	95
11. *Ryvita* Meal	101
12. Give and it will be Given unto You	109
13. Increased Faith	113
14. A Faith Challenge	117

15. How Lovely is Your Dwelling Place	123
16. God my Sufficiency	137
17. A New Season	143
18. Jean	151
19. Street Encounters	163
20. Years of Restoration	183
21. Dreams come True	193
22. Wind of Change	205
23. New Adventures	219
24. I Love to Dream	227
25. God's Spirit Beckons	237
26. Putting Down Roots	249
27. Gold Dust	259
28. Release of Joy	269
29. Polishing the Arrowhead	279
30. A Time of Moving On	287
31. What Next?	295
32. Dreams of Revival	307
33. A New Day Dawning	317
Final Points to Ponder	323

Dedication

I dedicate this book to all my family and friends both past and present who have influenced my walk of faith.

Acknowledgements

To Jesus Christ my Lord and Saviour for eternally changing my life.

Heartfelt thanks to Jona my wonderful husband for his constant encouragement and belief in me that I can do more than I think I can.

To Jenny my motivator, editor and friend, and to Jon-Jon my son for help and advice in publishing.

To Chelsea my granddaughter for her constant encouragement.

To Louisa for reigniting the spark in me to believe that writing the book is a God given inspiration.

To Karen, my American friend for all the fun memories we share.

To Chris, Mark, Stephen and Emily for their encouragements and endorsements of the book and finally to my wonderful Discipleship Group sisters and church family whose encouragements and prayers constantly sustain me.

I love you all.

Endorsements

Many of us will have experienced those hot, humid and sticky days, when we long for a cool breeze to blow; bringing that breath of fresh air that revives and renews our strength. Leadership and ministry within a local church setting can sometimes create a similar feeling; when we desire and pray for a fresh touch of God to ignite the tinder of the ongoing work of God's faithful people.

For me, having someone like Joy join the church was just that - a timely breath of fresh air! To encounter someone with a deep love and passion for the Lord, with the willingness to abandon their whole life into His hands in order to go deeper with Him in intimacy and service, is very special. It was a privilege and an honour to walk alongside Joy as mentor and friend, enjoying the breeze with her.

Joy's desire is to catch the breath of God, so she can give it away to others. Her love, energy and passion are infectious; stirring and inspiring those around her to step out in faith, to fly and soar in God's breeze.

'The Life of Joy' is an appropriate title!

Mark A Hatto
Minister
Emmanuel Baptist Church, Swanage, Dorset

It is easy to observe from the Bible that the name of a person is often a significant thing. With reference to Joy Jones she is definitely Joy by name and joy by nature! Read this gripping story of the life of Joy and be amazed and inspired to live your own life in the fullness of joy that only Jesus can give.

Rev'd Stephen Thompson
Bromham Baptist Church

Joy has an inspiring thirst and love for Jesus as well as a passion for people to know the Father's love for themselves. I wanted to find, feel, see and know if I could feel what Joy felt. Through time; The Alpha Course; fellowship; support and encouragement I was baptised in 2011 with Joy by my side. I know God's love for me and that I have eternal life through him and him alone.

Emily Prentice

Foreword

Do you need encouragement in your life? Read this book!

Joy writes like Joy talks - full of enthusiasm and faith with an innate ability to see God at work all around her and with the belief that God has an amazing plan for her life, although that hasn't always been the case for Joy.

Whether you believe there is a God or whether you're unsure, you will love reading the adventures of Joy as she shows how God can take an ordinary life and make it extraordinary. Read this book and you will be inspired to live a life of faith yourself.

Revd. Chris Duffett
Evangelist and founder of The Light Project.

Introduction

Zephaniah 3 verse 10
The Lord your God is with you, He is mighty to save.
He will take great delight in you. He will quiet you with his love,
He will rejoice over you with singing.

How wonderful it is to know that I am a joy to my Heavenly Father and that He delights in me.

It has taken me years, on a long spiritual journey to come to the realisation of this truth and find my true identity as who I am as a child of our Heavenly Father.

This book is about certain parts of that journey. My prayer is that as you read this book you too will come to the same realisation of Father's great personal love for you. Yes, He delights over you with singing!

This is my first attempt to write a book. It came about as the result of friends telling me I should do so. I love telling people about how great God has been in my life and in other people's lives too. I wrestled with the idea for some time, thinking there are so many good Christian books out there. What could I possibly write that people would want to read? Then I felt God speak to me and confirm the words through the mouth of a friend. 'People listen to what you say and they will read what you write.'

So here I am, inviting you to share my journey and life of joy!

Chapter 1

The Birth of Joy

Isaiah 49 verse 1
Before I was born the Lord called me; from my birth He has made mention of my name.

'You have another girl!' The midwife yelled as she hung her head out of the bedroom window to my father who was feverishly digging the garden. What a shock I was for them! They were convinced that God was going to bless them with a son. My parents had just survived the second-world war and already had two teenage daughters. Although both parents were in their

40's they decided to ask God to bless them with a son.

My father was a lay preacher and my mother had particularly wanted to give my father a son, who would follow in his footsteps in preaching the gospel.

Shortly after my birth my mother contracted pneumonia and was quite ill for some time. In retrospect I am putting the confusion in naming me (that I have heard all about) down to her illness. First they were going to call me Jennifer then decided against it when they heard someone else in the village had just named their baby girl Jennifer. Then came the bright idea to call me Joey, after all I was supposed to be Joseph. (Thank God I wasn't born in Australia!) No offence meant to anyone reading this who might be called Joey – but I think God had a merciful and divine hand in having the registrar miss out the 'e' and naming me Joy.

As I recall my childhood I would describe myself as a quirky child and quite withdrawn. Although I didn't realise it then, it was about my identity as the girl I wasn't supposed to be. By the time I was five years old my sisters were married, so in many ways I grew up an only child.

The surroundings of where I grew up were quite idyllic, a country cottage set in three quarters of an acre of ground that included an orchard that in summer was laden with luscious fruit.

From an early age I was a definite daddy's girl and wherever he was that is where I wanted to be. I have happy memories of trailing behind him, helping him in the garden, preparing beehives, feeding the pigs and hens. Although I wasn't always as keen on feeding the hens, because the cockerel seemed to be intent on attacking me whenever it clapped its eyes upon me. (It paid the price – we eventually ate it for Sunday lunch!)

My father was the village postman, which meant he would be up at 5.30 am for work. He would finish the post round mid morning then come home to work on running the smallholding that supplemented the family income. One of my favourite times of the day was after lunch when he would sit down for five minutes of shut-eye and I would climb on to his knee and snuggle up as he snoozed. I remember it as feeling the safest place in the world.

The early bonding I had with my mother wasn't as strong. She had little patience and was quite often stressed by the demands of life and there were many! She was caring for elderly parents, a sister who was chronically sick and frequently other people in the village who were unwell. As well as bringing up teenagers and me a little one, helping my father with work on the land and going through the menopause! Despite the demands upon her time our home was always filled with the sweet smells of clean laundry and delicious cooking – smells that linger in my memory today.

Starting school was definitely a culture shock for me! I was not used to socialising with other children apart from the ones I met at Sunday School. I have no recollection at all of my first day at school, the memories I have of infant school are of standing in the playground from where I could see my home. As I looked around at other children getting on with playing games, I would be standing alone gazing wistfully at our kitchen window wondering what my mother would be doing and wishing with all my heart that I could be there with her. Eventually reality hit me and I realised that school was now to be part of my life. Things that stick in my mind of those early days of school are of the class teacher Miss Asher, who always smelt nice and was always smiling and kind.

No sooner had I settled in to school before two other events took place that rocked my world. My sisters gave birth to baby boys within six months of each other. This brought big change for me as up to then at weekends I would sometimes go and stay with my eldest sister and enjoy time being the centre of her attention.

I have to say both she and her husband worked hard to make me feel included, involving me in buying things in preparation for the new baby and after he was born including me in choosing a name for him. My sister had come back home for the confinement, I recall the day my nephew was born as a lot of bustling about going on and eventually being told that I could go up and see my sister and her new baby. I have loving memories of how she snuggled me up on the bed beside her and discussed what we might name him.

I think I found it easier accepting the birth of my other nephew who had been born six months earlier as my sister had lived away from home since leaving school, so maybe I wasn't so emotionally attached to her. The strongest memories I have of my relationship with her in my early years are of before she was married and working away and coming home and bringing me presents. Particularly I remember a bag and a doll that she gave me.

Needless to say with new babies for my mother to focus her attention on, I guess I began to feel left out and as much as my sister tried to include me I felt I was no longer the centre of her attentions either. I do recall one dastardly thing I did in order to get some attention at the expense of my poor sister. It was a lovely hot summer day when they came over for tea, my sister was wearing a low cut sundress as was fashionable at the time. I waited until everyone had sat down and then dropped a harvest spider down her cleavage!

Pandemonium broke out, my sister in hysterics everyone jumping up from the table to the rescue! My father heading swiftly in my direction – I think any parenting skills he had departed from him in all the uproar. Instead of smacking me or sending me to my room he took the top off a tomato and put it down my back telling me it was a spider that would bite me. Enter a fear of spiders! Father, bless him, lived with the consequences of that action for the rest of his life. Many times afterwards, as I was growing up I would scream 'Spider' only to hear my mother yell to my father, 'Well it's your fault she's afraid of them so you can go deal with it.' Even in the last ten years of his life when he lived with us and suffered with Parkinson's disease there were times when he would have to come shakily to my rescue.

Looking back I think this was a landmark period in my young life. Fears and insecurities began to manifest; some of which are a normal part of childhood, I was frightened of the dark; frightened to go to bed; frightened of feathers and anything that fluttered (it was probably that cockerel!) and numerous other things too.

I also became quite phobic about anyone looking at me, I hated having my photograph taken and anything like school plays or Sunday School anniversaries where I had to stand in front of people would terrorise me. I would usually have to be carried from the platform in floods of tears. I recall one time when I locked myself in the pantry so that I would not have to perform in something. This exacerbated within me the feelings of being different and not like other children in that I could not bear to stand up in front of people let alone speak something out. It was as if the enemy knew one day I would be speaking out boldly for Jesus in public ministry. As an adult I came to realise that some of this was rooted in one of my mother's pet names for me. She would call me her 'little ugly duckling'.

Bless her, she had no idea of how that could and no doubt did, impact my self-esteem. To her it was a term of affection, as it was when she called me her 'little sausage.'

Chapter 2

Learning about Jesus

Proverbs 22 verse 6
Train a child in the way he should go and when he is old he will not turn from it.

My parents definitely believed that children are a gift from the Lord and so it was, I am told, that my first outing in the big wide world was to church for my parents to give thanks to God for my safe arrival. I do not personally remember the occasion but certainly do not recall a time in my young childhood when I wasn't taken to church.

Sunday routine was usually my father taking me to church with him in the morning whilst mother stayed home and cooked Sunday lunch. After lunch Father and I would be back to church for Sunday School, then in the evenings I would be taken along to the evening service with both parents. Generally speaking as a family we did little else on Sundays other than go to church. Sometimes in the summer we would go out for a walk in the countryside, but that was about it.

There came a time when I kicked my heels in rebellion against the above- mentioned Sunday routine. (More about that later.). However I find it interesting now to look back at those times from a different perspective. As a young child I delighted in spending a whole day with my father and have fond memories of walking home from church on Sunday mornings, holding his hand and chatting, sometimes about what I had heard said in church.

Another regular happening on a Sunday morning was my uncle would always be there when we got in from church and leave soon after we arrived home. I would always be asking him to stay longer, but his reply was always the same: 'It was time for him to go to his church.' This puzzled me for some time, eventually as I got older I found out he meant the pub!

I have happy and treasured memories of snuggling up next to my mother in church on Sunday evenings, feeling the warmth from her body, enjoying the scent of her perfume and feeling safe and secure. It was a time when I was guaranteed to have my mother to myself – apart from the distraction of the preacher. I was content not to be allowed verbal communication with her in what I now realise was a precious time of togetherness and bonding. So it was from early days I was saturated in biblical truth and acceptance that attending church services on

Sundays were the most important events of the week.

From a young age I was a people-watcher with an inquisitive mind. From all I heard, I knew I went to Sunday School to learn about Jesus and we went to church to worship God – whatever that meant?

I was intrigued by people who went to church, some when you met them in the week would seem to be different people to who they were in church, some were just the same and would talk about God and Jesus in a most natural way. It was these people who intrigued me the most and who I would love to be around: they caused my young heart to want to know God and Jesus like they did.

Apart from my parents another person who influenced my life spiritually was my father's sister, my Aunt Edie. She was a spinster who lived with my granddad caring for him in his old age. Despite having a disability (she was left paralysed in one leg after contracting polio as a toddler), she was always cheerful and full of fun. I remember her coming to visit me cheering me up and making me laugh when I was in bed with some childhood illness. She always had so much love to pour out as well as stories. Whenever I saw her she would have a Jesus story to tell me, either a story from the Bible or a tale to tell about some adventure that she had had with Jesus.

There was also a local preacher who stands out in my memory, Mr. Till, who would occasionally come to preach at our church. I would eagerly look forward to him coming to have tea with us because he always spent time chatting with me. I have a vivid memory of one visit when I would be about five or six years old and I was playing with my Teddy bear and dolls, putting them to bed in my dolls' cot when Mr. Till asked me what I wanted to do when I was grown up. I said, 'Be a nurse.' I think the reason that conversation has stuck in my mind is because of the kindness and interest shown towards me that was demonstrated through the question.

My favourite times at Sunday School were when we had missionaries come to speak to us. I loved to hear their stories about how they travelled to foreign lands to tell people about how much Jesus loved them. It was when I was only five or six years old that we had a lady from The China Inland Mission come to speak to us about the work she did with children in China. It was then that I decided in my childlike way that I wanted to be like her. I wanted to know Jesus like she knew him and I wanted to tell everyone about him. All day the things she had spoken about and the gospel message she had given played on my mind. That evening as my father was walking out of my bedroom after tucking me up in bed for the night I told him I wanted to be like her and I wanted Jesus to live in my heart. He came over to me and prayed a childlike prayer of salvation with me.

My own spiritual journey had commenced!

Chapter 3

Getting to know Jesus

Matthew 4 verse 19

'Come follow me,' Jesus said, 'and I will make you fishers of men.'

I have no doubt the conversion experience I had the night when my father prayed with me was real. From that point on I had a childlike understanding in my heart that Jesus was my Saviour who loved me, that He had died to forgive my sins and when I died I would go to Heaven to be with Him forever.

Looking back now I can see how God was at work forming desires and appreciations in me that many years later He would fulfil.

Growing up in the country I developed a love for nature and the outdoors. I have fond memories of warm summer days and running through fields of cowslips, taking walks in the country side with my aunt as she taught me about nature and told me some of her Jesus stories. We had such fun times that I now realise were foundational in me becoming a worshipper of our creator God.

The times I recall being some of the happiest as a child were when I was alone outdoors with God. One of my favourite places was on my swing which hung from a large old apple tree in the garden. It was here I would talk to Jesus about many things and dream of one day preaching and telling people how much Jesus loved them and that He wanted them to go to Heaven to be with him when they died. My dolls and Teddy bear were my attentive congregation. (That scene came vividly back to my mind in recent years when I was visiting a friend who was Pastor of a church in Kenya. We had trekked some distance to visit some villagers and as I sat on a low wall with several youths listening to me tell them about Jesus I recalled the little girl preaching to her dolls.) Often times when I was playing in the garden I would hear my paternal grandfather singing hymns or spiritual songs at the top of his voice as he worked in the garden.

A bit of background on my paternal grandfather: his wife, my grandmother died before I was born. He lived with my fun-filled aunty although they could not have been more different in personality. I remember him as being rather an austere character. When I went to visit them there were times when speaking was strictly prohibited. When granddad was reading his Bible or listening to the news on the radio I had to be as quiet as a mouse or I knew I would be in trouble and he would holler at me. His softer side would come out when I sometimes stayed overnight when he would always bring aunty and me a cup of tea and a biscuit in bed before we got up in the morning. I saw it again as I got a bit older when every Friday night he would give me a threepenny bit for a bag of chips.

A particular amusing memory I have of him working in the garden was watching him as he was trying with all his might to pull up a tall stubborn weed out of the ground. All of a sudden it came out and he went flying backwards, weed, arms and legs all flying in the air. The sight was hilarious and caused me to roar with laughter much to my grandfather's disgust, I wasn't sure who he was angry at most, me or the weed! So I ran for cover whilst he regained his composure.

As I have already said he was often heard to be singing songs and one of his favourites went 'I need thee, oh! I need thee, every hour I need thee.' Maybe it was from listening to his singing that I developed a love for expressing my own heart to God through song.

One of my favourite childhood choruses that I loved to sing was 'I will make you fishers of men if you follow me.' I remember singing it with gusto as my heart responded to the words, feeling all I wanted to do was follow Jesus and tell people about him. Looking back I see that the Holy Spirit planted the words of the song in my heart and used them to create within me a desire for evangelism, that, Praise God, I still have today. In a childlike way I developed a genuine concern for the eternal well-being of my young school friends and recall witnessing to one in particular, explaining to her how when we die we go to either Heaven or Hell and the choice of where we go is up to us. To my knowledge she never responded to my preaching any more than my dolls did! I guess I was thought of as being somewhat weird. I was different, and was made to feel different as other children at school often excluded me from their games and friendship circles.

It was, however, such times that taught me the value of kindness and compassion. I knew what it was to feel lonely and isolated and I could discern when others were feeling that way too and would seek to befriend them. There was a particularly neglected child who came to school very unkempt and who no one would want to play with. I recall feeling her pain of rejection and her delight as I became her friend and we would skip round the playground together. Although my mother was not so delighted in my choice of friends as it meant her having the job of delousing my long hair every night, much to my objections!

I had discovered everything that I had heard about Jesus to be true. He became my best friend, I would talk to Him about everything and I increasingly wanted to share His love with the world.

Then came adolescence.

Chapter 4

The Years of Change

Genesis 4 verse 7
... if you do not do what is right, sin is crouching at your door ...

I recall my adolescent years as being a most confused and painful time of many changes.

My parents, being older and with quite a Victorian outlook to life, had not prepared me for the onset of puberty. Such things were just not spoken about. So all of a sudden I found changes taking place in my body and changes taking place in the warm and affectionate relationship I had always shared with my father. Although he was kind and cheerful towards me as usual, I no longer received the hugs and cuddles that I had once been used to. The explanation I was given was that I was growing up in to a big girl and with that explanation came a kind of unspoken understanding that I wasn't a child any more so I was too big to sit on my father's knee. I was 11.

Another massive change for me was moving up to secondary school. This proved to be a bigger culture shock to me than when I had started school in the first place. I could no longer see my home from the school playground. Instead I had to travel each day on a school bus to the secondary school that was in a town two and a half miles from where we lived.

The school was also a lot bigger than I had been used to as it took in children from several other outlying villages. As well as me adapting to there being a lot more children around, there were school showers to contend with too!! These became a real anathema to me! It was bad enough that I found the whole experience embarrassing. But when I saw other girls bare all in the shower I began to compare myself with some of their curvy shapes and felt myself severely lacking. The only big things I had were my size seven feet. Was I really my mother's ugly duckling?

It is in retrospect I can see as my insecurities increased particularly concerning body image, the enemy of my soul was lying in waiting. Craving attention and acceptance, I so wanted to be part of the in-crowd of girls who always appeared to be cool and popular with everyone. Observing their way of life, which was so different from my own, it seemed to be attractive and exciting to me. As I began to hang around with them I was introduced to a catalogue of new interests: make-up, secular music, smoking and boys!

Home life became a battle-field of arguments with my parents. I recall the first time that I dabbled with makeup. After spending ages before the bathroom mirror seemingly making myself beautiful with eye shadow and lipstick, I emerged to meet my father face to face as he was waiting to use the bathroom! Shock horror was all over his face! I was marched to the sink and made to scrub it all off and was told never to try it again. Needless to say I did and we had more fights about the rights and wrongs of wearing make-up. At the time I thought my father to be an old fashioned misery, little did I know that I was increasingly distancing myself from the love and protection of my parents through my own rebellion.

Some of the secular music that I listened to at the time certainly helped fuel the rebellion and increase the feelings of rejection in me. I remember one particular song with the words 'nobody loves me I'm nobody's child' in it.

Obviously I didn't understand it at the time, but can now see clearly how the enemy used those words to sow lies into my spirit as I began to believe them to be true.

Looking back I realise that it was a time when there was intense spiritual warfare going on over my life. Frequently I would be singing some slushy secular love song and I would think of Jesus and sing it to him and feel such love for him. I believe worship to God always pains the ears of the enemy and as he saw the potential in the worshipping heart of a young person, the battle for my soul intensified.

I became more engaged in the activities of my new-found friends and would sometimes sneak out of school with them at lunchtime to go into town, where we would hang out in the local café and listen to records on the juke box while checking out the local talent.

My father, in trying to reach out to me and salvage something of our relationship, bought me a bicycle and taught me to ride it. Alas, it was as though I was out of reach. Although I spent many happy hours on sunny days going off on long cycle rides in the countryside with one of my friends from primary school days. I would also use it as a means of transport to go behind my parents' backs and meet my friends from the café. By the time I was 14 I had developed a keen interest in the opposite sex and was delighted when boys began showing an interest in me. This made me feel that I was accepted and really was one of the crowd.

Rebellion increased; I no longer sang love songs to Jesus but would be dreaming about some boy or other. I refused to go to church and argued with my parents about everything. My beloved elder sister, who I usually had so much respect for, tried to point out to me the slippery slope that I was on but this was to no avail: I thought she had become an old fashioned misery and spoilsport just like my parents!

I became one of the coolest girls in the crowd (or so I thought) when a guy who was some six years older than me asked me out and started dating me in a serious way. Needless to say, much to the relief of my family I am sure, the relationship fizzled out after a few months. However the path that I had chosen to take that I thought to be cool and exciting turned out to be a rapid descent in to an abyss of unhappiness and chaos that I would live in for several years to come.

Any dreams I had had of being a missionary or a preacher were forgotten about and lost along the way, although for a while I hung on to the desire to become a nurse. For my parents this was a non-starter as it meant I would have to move away from home. They were already frantic enough about my behaviour without me moving from their sight! I left school when I was 15 without any qualifications, this being mainly due to me being more interested in boys rather than getting an education. So it was on leaving school that I drifted in to the retail trade. Drifting is a good word to describe how I felt at the time. I felt like I was lost and alone in the middle of an ocean, not knowing who I was, what I was doing or where I was going.

From that point on for several years I drifted from one relationship to another and lurched from one disaster to another.

Chapter 5

Lost at Sea

John 10 verse 10
The thief comes only to steal and kill and destroy...

The next fifteen years of my life I can only describe as being storm tossed on the sea of life.

I didn't enjoy working in the retail trade at all and so it was I began to dream about white weddings, getting married and having children. The dream was in sight when I started dating a young man who my parents approved of. He was a year older than me and the relationship was encouraged. We became engaged to be married, when at 17 I discovered that I was pregnant! Any fairy tale dreams I had had of romantic white weddings quickly evaporated as plans were rapidly made for us to have a quiet chapel wedding. Looking back it is as if we were caught up in a whirlwind, one event followed another. We had felt so grown up and valued the freedom we had found from parental control. Whilst we were floundering in the new found responsibilities of married life and running a home, five months into the marriage and six weeks before my eighteenth birthday I gave birth two months prematurely to a baby boy. Any joy I felt at becoming a mother quickly turned to sorrow as I was told that our baby was not going to make it in this world and was asked if we would like to have him christened. In our absence he was christened Mark Peter and died six hours later. He was laid to rest in the church graveyard that was local to the hospital.

Following this traumatic event I recall rolling between feelings of numbness and utter emptiness and loss, my arms aching to hold and love the baby we had lost. I do not recall ever having any feelings of anger towards God for what had happened, just the pain of loss. I did though occasionally wonder if God was punishing me for not living according to his ways.

Although I had turned my back on wanting to live for God I continually prayed from the yearnings of my heart that He would give me another baby to love and to hold in my empty arms. Well-meaning friends would sympathise with us and tell us not to rush things reminding us we were young and had plenty of time to have children. However, my prayers were answered and after seven months I became pregnant again. Little did I realise at the time that there was wisdom in the advice of our friends. Being young, neither of us understood that we each needed to come to terms with and work through the pain of losing a child. In reality we were little more than children ourselves.

Although I was thrilled to be pregnant again, the trauma of losing our first child etched fresh in my mind and I spent most of the pregnancy in a state of anxiety. I so wanted this baby to be OK.

Again things did not go straight forward: I went in to premature labour again, this time at eight months and gave birth to another baby boy. It was a couple of weeks before I got to bring him home and hold him in my arms. I had had to leave him in hospital because of his prematurity until he was deemed well enough to survive. I was traumatised (although I did not realise it at the time) my dreams of giving birth to a healthy thriving baby had been shattered: I had initially come home from hospital again experiencing empty arms syndrome. Then when I finally brought the tiny little cherub home he wouldn't feed and I knew only too well we were at crisis for his survival and vividly recall sitting by the fireside with him in my arms, constantly trying to get him to feed with tears streaming down my cheeks and spending the whole night crying out to God 'Please don't let my baby die.' (I am happy to report God answered my prayer!) I found out later that the midwife had told my sister that the baby did not stand a chance of survival!

They were not easy days for sure! My parents had moved away, so had one of my sisters and the sister who lived close by had her own problems to contend with, caring for an elderly mother-in-law and then herself being diagnosed with cancer. Looking back I can see how gracious God was to me as although I did not have practical support from close family, people in the village rallied around me and came and helped out, giving me loving support and advice that I was in desperate need of.

Getting married and having children did not seem to be working out to be the exciting dream I thought it would be. Four years into our marriage I gave birth to our third child, another baby boy. Despite a difficult breach birth, he was born healthy and quickly thrived. However, as much as I loved our children there was this constant feeling of emptiness within me and a craving to be loved and to experience some excitement in my life.

The feelings of emptiness within me were exacerbated when one my sisters migrated to Australia with her husband and family. I felt the loss of her company acutely. This was soon followed by an even greater loss to me, when my beloved older sister lost her fight against cancer and died at the age of forty two. It was like the bottom had dropped out of my world.

I recall telling God that I did not understand how He could allow this to happen to my sister, she was a good person and was happily married with two children, I questioned why wasn't it me, since I was so miserable.

I was desperately unhappy in my marriage and now had no one to whom I could turn for help. My parents and brother-in-law, who I was very close to, were all far too locked in their own grief to notice my pain. All the traumatic events that had taken place in our marriage had taken their toll and instead of turning to each other, we had both turned to other forms of comfort, so after eight years of marriage it finally ended in divorce.

I suppose in my naivety I thought when I walked away from my marriage I had walked away from unhappiness. The truth was that I took it with me. I discovered the unhappiness I felt in the marriage was largely the result of me feeling unhappy within myself. Nothing in life seemed to be plain-sailing. With the divorce came the added responsibility of being the sole provider for two children.

I eventually rented us a one-bedroom flat that was in an old Victorian house that had been converted in to several flats and bedsits, where goodness knows how many of us, shared the one bathroom and toilet. However we all lived in harmonious community and cared for one another. I soon found part time work to help support us, which of course meant I needed to find a child minder to look after the children whilst I was at work. Amazingly I found one who lived only a few doors down in the same street as us and was able to place the children with her. Little did I know that meeting that particular child minder would bring about a chain of events in my life that would lead to finding long term happiness and contentment beyond my wildest dreams.

Point to ponder: In times of trauma and pain where do you turn for comfort?

One of the names of the Holy Spirit is Comforter – He loves you and is always there to comfort you.

Chapter 6

Outpouring of God's Kindness

A chain of events began to unfold when one day the child minder introduced me to her handsome brother and fixed us up to go out on a date.

I was quite enjoying my newly found freedom and all the hedonistic pleasures that came with it. All thoughts of my relationship with God were pushed deep, deep down and hidden away, or so I thought!

Then came the arranged date with the child minder's brother! This was supposed to be just another date, a quiet drink in a pub and maybe a bit of fun to follow.

God was far from my thoughts, so you can imagine the shock I had when sitting in the pub, enjoying a quiet drink, he steered the conversation around to finish up telling me that when he was younger, he used to be quite religious and had been quite actively involved in church life! What? Why did he go and tell me all that about himself? These were the thoughts running through my mind.

Of course I empathically interjected in the conversation with nods of agreement and understanding, informing him that I too had come from a similar place!

There was a disturbance in my spirit – I knew God was on my case! This was turning out to be no ordinary date.

What followed I am sure was no ordinary relationship either! Drawn together by some kind of kindred spirit we became inseparable. I was drawn like a moth to a flame as he would play his guitar and sing spiritual songs to me. My fellow housemates all got on well with him and he was soon accepted as one of the crowd.

Unfortunately our parents were not as accepting of our developing relationship. My parents, despairing of what I was getting myself in to now and his parents distraught because their son was seriously dating a divorced woman with two children.

At the time I am sure neither set of parents could see God's hand at work in our lives, but unmistakably it was! Their opposition to our relationship only fuelled the rebellious streak that we both had and consequently drew us closer to each other and made the relationship even stronger.

One day not long into our relationship out of the blue, my strange new man dropped another of his little quips and suggested I go to church on Sunday. He had to be joking! He wasn't, and explained to me there was going to be a special service to say goodbye to one of his older brothers who was going to live abroad to be a missionary.

I laugh as I recall it now – surely I must have had brain freeze or something, as I agreed to go and did not question why he wanted me to go, yet didn't want to go himself!

God had set me up to have my spirit disturbed some more! I went along to the service to please my man with the expectation of receiving condemnation – this was not to be. I was totally disturbed by the whole experience – here was a man with his wife and three children who had given up everything, a good job and a nice home to go and serve God in missions. Was he crazy?

Thinking of my own living conditions, I found it hard to comprehend, and very challenging that someone would give up all that security and comfort.

Then the unthinkable – when I was leaving after the service realising who I was, Big Brother introduced himself to me, bracing myself for what might come next, I was totally shocked to hear him say that he was pleased to meet me and wanted me to know that he did not judge me! It wasn't just the words that shocked me; I actually felt a genuine unconditional love and acceptance from the man.

I pondered over in my mind, 'Is this guy crazy or is God really worth giving everything up for?' In my heart I knew the answer to this question but resisted facing up to it and so it was that I spent the next three years of my life in turmoil of mind and heart, as I wrestled with the question that would not go away.

Big Brother went off abroad with his family and we jollied along in our relationship. I suppose this may be the right time to say that by saying 'we' I am referring to Jona and me. Yes, even his name was different – pronounced Jona as opposed to Jonah, though at the time, the latter may have been more appropriate. I found out actually that he had been christened Jonathan but for some reason he had a vehement dislike to the name.

After a few months Jona moved in to live with us. Neither of us spoke to each other about any spiritual conviction that may have been going on in our hearts, although increasingly I was recognising and appreciating that he was a man of spiritual strength. This was really affirmed when tragedy struck our community, a young couple living upstairs from us lost a baby girl quite suddenly in a matter of hours to Meningococcal Meningitis. The whole community was racked in grief and when Jona and I were alone, I threw the questions I had about God right at him – 'Where was God in all this?' 'How could he let such a thing happen?' He did not pretend to understand or have an answer, yet somehow displayed a spiritual strength to us all that kind of said, we have to trust God even when we do not understand things that are going on around us. Maybe that was the time when I truly felt I want this man to be part of my life forever.

Another person who was a strength and spiritual influence to me personally and to all of us sharing the house was Dennis, a local Minister. Looking back now it is clear that he was God's strategically placed instrument in that season of my life.

Although I was trying to ignore my own childhood experiences of church, I wanted my own children to learn the spiritual truths that I had learnt as a child and so sent them to Sunday School at Dennis' church.

Over a period of two years he became a true friend and Minister and was a constant in the life of our little community; he constantly demonstrated the most amazing unconditional love to us all. I do not recall him ever passing one word of judgement towards us about our chosen life-style; rather he regularly visited us, listened to our stories, gave us comfort and advice and was not opposed to rolling up his sleeves and giving practical help when it was needed.

He was a wise man with a shepherd's heart for the lost and now I realise also had a keen eye for recognising sheep that had gone astray! I recall him one day challenging me to consider the possibility that I could have a relationship with God as well as with Jona. The challenge was met with a blank response!

It was a loss to us all when Dennis moved out of the area to be Minister in a church several miles away.

Two years in to our relationship I became pregnant and gave birth to another son. When I had discovered that I was pregnant we had no idea how we would manage for space; we had moved in to a slightly bigger one bedroom flat when one became vacant in the house but we were still overcrowded. The boys had the bedroom and we slept in the lounge that we used as a bed/sitting room.

Like most of us living in the house at the time I had my name down on the local council housing list and so went and explained to them the situation we found ourselves in. I was given assurance that when the child was born we would be given somewhere suitable to live.

It turned out that they were true to their word! I recall vividly the day I sent Jona to inform the council that the baby had arrived, thinking at least it would get things in motion towards getting us re-housed. Imagine my amazement as I sat there holding our son only a couple of days old and Jona came in and waved a set of keys in my face! More amazement quickly followed when I found out that we had been given a brand new house with three bedrooms, a bathroom and two toilets! A week later we had moved in to what to us felt like a mansion.

Chapter 7

Saved by Grace

Ephesians 2 verses 8-9

For it is by grace you have been saved, through faith – and this is not from yourselves, it is the gift of God – not by works, so that no one can boast.

We were overjoyed with the luxury of our new home. The location was perfect: it was situated on the edge of a newly-built housing estate facing open countryside and although our furnishings were sparse we were so happy to have a brand new home we could call our own.

My happiness was only marred by one thing – that was the displeasure all of our parents demonstrated towards us because we were living together as a family and was not married. In the eyes of our parents we were living in sin.

Whilst Jona's parents would make remarks, it was the lectures I would get from my mother every time we went to visit my parents that were the most painful to me. She would never challenge Jona or say anything to me in front of him but would always manage to get me on my own and then I would be given a good talking to!

I knew she was ashamed of me and of my choice of life-style, what she didn't realise was, that with every lecture I was feeling increasingly more ashamed of myself too. Eventually it came to the point where I could not take any more of the condemnation I was feeling and told Jona what was going on. Up to this point I had never mentioned to him the hard times my mother was giving me. He was amazed as I poured out my heart to him about how I felt inside. He had let remarks made to him by his parents just roll off his back and had had no idea of how my sensitive spirit was suffering from an overload of condemnation.

Jona's solution to my distress was to ask me to marry him. Initially I was apprehensive to give a positive response thinking that he may have proposed to me as a means of expressing sympathy towards me. However I soon realised he was sincere about the proposal and wanted to make an honest woman of me and care for me and protect me and my children; and after all wasn't this what I was looking for and so I said 'Yes'.

Needless to say my parents were delighted when they heard the news. Although my father had never reprimanded me the way my mother had, I knew he had been disappointed with me and in his own quiet way would have been praying about my situation.

The response of my future in-laws to our news was to want to organize the wedding for us. This was something that did not go down well with either one of us, especially when they began to talk of us getting married in church! This led to Jona and me sitting down and having a serious discussion about what each of us was feeling and thinking. The outcome was that we were in agreement in several areas; whilst we appreciated all the help being offered us we both felt strongly this was our journey in life, it was our wedding, and we wanted to do it our way and plan it ourselves. We discovered we both also had a strong sense of authenticity and integrity about being true to ourselves. We wanted our wedding to be a reflection of who we really were and we did not see ourselves as church people. We informed his parents of our decision and so it was we spent the summer of 1977 planning a November wedding. We had little money but much happiness, we saved and took the children on a camping holiday and bought the essentials we needed for the wedding, new clothes for us all, wedding rings and planned for our big day.

We agreed that we would get married in the local registry office and that we would be unconventional and, with his employer's permission, we would decorate and drive to our wedding in the Volvo F88 tractor unit he drove for a living. Not being able to afford a wedding reception we decided on inviting friends and family to join us afterwards for a drink at a nearby working men's club. Our friends rallied around us and supported our plans, although some questioned why we were getting married, warning that marriage can change things. When the big day came all went according to plan until after the ceremony when we went to the working men's club to meet up with our friends for a drink. When we walked in we had the surprise of our lives and so did our family when we discovered our friends had all clubbed together secretly and had hired a room there and laid on a full wedding reception for us – complete with a three tier, pink iced, heart shaped wedding cake! What a wonderful day they made it for us. Wearing a floor length, light blue denim dress that was trimmed with white lace I felt like a princess as I danced enveloped in the arms of my husband. We had laughed at our friends who had said about marriage bringing change yet no sooner than we were married did some major change take place!

We had only been married for three weeks when 'Big Brother' returned home on furlough from his mission. Just as he had three years earlier, Jona again suggested that I go to church to hear his brother preach. This time my response was 'I will if you will!' I was only too aware of how disturbed I felt within myself from the last time I had gone to hear him preach, although I didn't tell Jona that. My thinking was 'What's good for the goose is good for the gander.'

So it was arranged that on a particular evening we would go to church together and his brother even arranged a lift for us. I could not believe what happened next – five minutes before our lift was due Jona was called in to work to take out a long distance load! It appeared the gander had escaped and the goose was going to have to go it alone. So much for my plans!

I went off to church not thinking about God, or how disturbed I had felt last time I went. I was consumed with annoyance regarding Jona's work and that he had got out of going; as far as I was concerned he was off on a jolly and I felt set up.

I sat in the back of the church stewing in my annoyance, not paying much attention to what was being said from the pulpit when suddenly my attention was grabbed by two verses of scripture being read from the authorized version of the Bible.

> Ephesians 2 verses 8-9.
>
> For by grace are ye saved through faith; and that not of yourselves: it is the gift of God: Not of works, lest any man should boast.

All of a sudden it was as though I was unaware of anything else that was being said or even other people being present in the church – I was alone with God. I *had* been set up – it was time to talk! I confessed that I recognised I had been thoroughly unhappy ever since I turned away from following Him as a child and had made a complete shambles of my life. I was ashamed of the way I had rebelled against Him and found it almost impossible to believe that He would welcome me back with open arms knowing all I had done. This was the first honest conversation I had had with God in years and I knew I could not go on without Him being in charge of my life. Somehow the scripture that had impacted me became alive to me. I knew that I did not deserve anything from God yet he was asking me to trust Him and receive His grace and forgiveness. My response to Him was 'I give myself totally back to you – I cannot fight you any longer, if you can do something with my life then do it.' I wanted to know the joy and peace I had known as a child when Jesus was my best friend. For the first time in years I knew real peace in my heart; I knew a transaction had taken place. I had given God all my wretchedness and brokenness and He had taken it and replaced it with a deep sense of peace and forgiveness.

When the service ended I didn't want to talk to anyone. All I wanted to do was to get home to be alone with God and process what had taken place in my heart, however it was arranged that family and friends would go back to my parents-in-law for supper. This turned out to be for me like something from a pantomime scene. One person I did not want to have a conversation with was Big Brother – I suppose I thought he might ask me about what I had thought of the service and that was a question I wasn't ready to answer. The room was full of people so I reckoned that I could easily avoid being drawn in to conversation with him. Wrong! I worked my way around the room engaging myself in small-talk with various people but every time I turned round he was there behind me, waiting to pounce! Eventually I think he got fed up of playing my game and announced to all and sundry that he and I would go in to the kitchen and make drinks!

Once we got in the kitchen he closed the door and placed his hands firmly upon my shoulders and asked me if I knew Jesus as my Lord and Saviour. I confidently replied 'Yes, I do.' then he asked 'And since when?' Drat the man!! 'Since tonight!' I confessed. The story of what had happened in the service rolled from my lips; much to his elation I might add! He had been very much aware that God had been at work! I was in tears and shared with him how terrified I felt regarding what Jona's reaction would be to my news. I had been through one divorce and never wanted to go through another. He assured me that I wouldn't and that his brother would understand. With all my heart I hoped he was right!

The evening turned into a celebration of my re-commitment to declaring not only Jesus as my Saviour as I had done as a child, but as Lord of my entire life! I sincerely wanted Him to take full control of the life I had so badly messed up and He did. Just like the story of the prodigal son in Luke 15 I had come to my senses and returned home to the Father's house.

That was 11th December 1977.

Point to ponder: When we surrender all to Christ, that includes our shame as well, so we can walk free.

Chapter 8

Repent and be Baptised

> Acts 2 verse 38
> Peter replied, 'Repent and be baptised, every one of you, in the name of Jesus Christ for the forgiveness of your sins. And you will receive the Holy Spirit.'

Following that eventful Sunday evening I had almost a whole week to wait and stew over what I was going to say to Jona when he returned home from the long distance trip. I decided it was not the kind of thing I wanted to tell him over the telephone and opted for telling him to his face when he came home the following Friday evening. I greeted him home having prepared him a lovely steak dinner to soften the blow and with some trepidation broke the news to him about my re-commitment to Jesus. I waited with baited breath for the response, not knowing what to expect. I was pleasantly surprised to hear him say that he was really pleased for me regarding the decision I had made and then added a caveat that although he was pleased for me - I was not to preach to him!

A new way of life had begun for me. Before Big Brother returned to his mission base he introduced me to some local Christians who were part of a newly formed house church in my local area, where I was quickly embraced as part of the church family. The change in my life-style was so radical. I had an insatiable appetite for reading the Bible and went to church at every opportunity and wanted to tell everyone my story of how good God is.

My changed life-style, enthusiasm and newfound love for Jesus resulted in three ladies in the local neighbourhood asking me questions about what had happened to me. Consequently this led them to accept Jesus as their own personal Saviour too. We were all hungry to learn more about the things of God. It was not unusual for us to gather together at my home almost on a daily basis to pray, listen to teaching tapes and study the Bible.

One thing I had quickly decided upon was that I wanted to be obedient to Jesus' teaching and profess my faith publicly through baptism by total immersion. Remembering the faithful love our Minister friend Dennis had shown us before he moved away. I decided if at all possible I would like him to be the one who baptised me. So after discussion with my church Elders I contacted Dennis and told him my news and asked him the question. Needless to say he was delighted with my news and invited Jona and me to go and stay with him and his wife for a weekend to plan the baptismal service. I could never have imagined what a blessing that weekend would turn out to be for us!

On route to visit Dennis we called in to see my parents. Whilst we were there Jona disappeared for several minutes. I didn't think anything of it until when we were back on the road and he pulled off saying he had something to say to me. I wondered what on earth it could be that was so important that he had had to pull of the road to tell me. To the delight of my ears, he told me that whilst at my parents he had taken himself off to the bathroom, got down on his knees and recommitted his own life to Jesus! I had noticed a few changes going on in Jona's life but had felt it best not to say anything to him. I noticed that pictures he always had of pin-up girls in his truck were no longer there and then the Bible he had used as a teenager had mysteriously vanished off the bookshelf. I had sincerely hoped these were all signs that God was at work in his life and indeed now my hopes had been confirmed. What a weekend of celebration we had!

One morning a couple of weeks prior to my baptism my three friends were round when we had an extraordinary manifestation of God's presence. We had gathered together in my front room listening to a worship tape, sent to me by my dear Aunt Edie, when suddenly the room was filled with the presence of God! Although there was no window open a gentle breeze blew through the room, I recall feeling as though I had been hit in the chest by something. We were all filled with mixed emotions, overwhelming joy, laughter and tears, behaving like drunken women. Then one the ladies started speaking in a foreign language. We had no idea what was going on, when just precisely at the right moment there was a knock at the front door and it was one of the church elders. He had come round as part of my baptism preparation to explain about the gifts of the Holy Spirit and how they work. He was shocked to find that God had kind of beaten him to it and had just demonstrated the teaching to us. We were greatly relieved to find out when he read to us from Acts 2 that what we had just experienced was an outpouring of the Holy Spirit as on the day of Pentecost and was in keeping with scripture.

The big day finally came around when I celebrated with family and friends as Dennis came and baptised me. Jona had been baptised as a teenager and used the occasion to renew his baptismal vows as a profession of his recommitment to God; and to celebrate us now being united in faith we also chose the occasion to have our marriage blessed. What a day!

I know baptism is an outward expression of an inward change that has already taken place but I will always remember coming out from the water feeling white and pure as though every bit of my sinful past had been washed off me and to be sure it had!

Chapter 9

A New Creation

> 2 Corinthians 5 verse 17
> Therefore, if anyone is in Christ, he is a new creation; the old has gone, the new has come!

The old me really had gone: it was as if I had been born again and given a brand new life! I could certainly appreciate the terminology of 'Born Again Christians', this really was my experience.

Like a newborn baby would hunger after a mother's milk, I hungered with an insatiable appetite for spiritual food. Fortunately I was in a church where there was good teaching and so was nurtured well in those early days.

I became close friends with an American girl who attended the same church; due to her husband being based over here with the American Air Force. She was very influential in encouraging me and mentoring me and enabled me to grow quite quickly in my newly found walk of faith. She would come round to my home and do Bible studies with me and she also took me to Bible study meetings on the local American airbase where I was able to meet and fellowship with other Christian women. These meetings were such fun times where we would study God's Word, pray for each other's needs and share our hopes, dreams and recipes. For me it was a great cultural learning experience as I learned more about the American way of life as well as it being a spiritual learning experience. It seemed that everything American was big: big cars, big homes, big furniture, big refrigerators and I would have to say big hearts! Through the times I spent with these precious ladies I came to understand more about the empowering of the Holy Spirit and how He operates in our lives, blessing us with gifts that enable us to live effective Christian lives.

It was during this period that I one day experienced something I would describe as an open vision. I was sitting in my front room relaxing, spending time with God, gazing out of the window and looking across the road at the beautiful sight of ripe golden coloured corn blowing in the harvest field. Suddenly I could see a group of women who all appeared to be of different nationalities, each one wearing national costume. All were in a circle, dancing in abandonment and worshipping God. In particular there was an Asian lady wearing a bright emerald green sari trimmed with gold that sparkled and glistened as it caught the rays of the glorious sunshine. Somehow she seemed to stand out from all the rest.

This was a totally new experience for me and as you can imagine I did a lot of pondering with God as to what on earth it could mean. It was quite soon after this when I was at a meeting on the airbase when one of the ladies began to tell me about a women's ministry called 'Women's Aglow' (now known simply as 'Aglow'). She handed me a leaflet about it and to my great astonishment on the front of it was a picture of a circle of women all of different nationalities! I immediately knew in my spirit that this was somehow connected with the vision that I'd had. I think the ladies were as surprised as me when I told them about the vision and how I had been pondering on its meaning. I found out that it was a ministry founded by a lady in America; that it was fast becoming international and was just being introduced in the UK, largely through the Christian women from the American airbases.

Realising that God was drawing our attention to this ministry we spent the next few weeks and months seeking whether He was in fact calling us to launch this ministry in our local area of the UK. Feeling strongly that this was the case we then contacted the National Board for the UK and after going through a prayerful process with them a 'Women's Aglow' chapter was launched in our local area.

It was a very exciting and challenging time that followed. I took on the role in serving as President of it, along with a team of awesome women of God, serving alongside me.

What really blessed me was that it was an inter-denominational ministry. Women from different church backgrounds could come together and enjoy fellowship over food, and invite their friends to come along and hear testimonies of how Jesus can change lives.

At the time my husband was also involved and serving in a very similar outreach ministry to men – the FGB (Full Gospel Business Men's Fellowship).

God certainly used the time that we served in these ministries to teach us so much about the faith walk as we sat under the inspired teaching of faith- filled men and women of God. We heard how our Father God is

Jehovah Jireh - The Lord God our provider, and began to learn how to trust Him for our daily needs.

Chapter 10

Food Provided

There are a few testimonies that spring to mind that really were stepping stones or building blocks in deepening our faith walk. Many times when struggling to make our finances stretch we would pray and see God meet our needs in the most amazing ways.

On one occasion we were totally out of food and after eating breakfast the cupboard was bare apart from tea bags. As a mother I was desperate; I knew the two older children would be OK at lunchtime as they had cooked dinners at school; but as to what the toddler and I were going to eat, I had no idea! Our faith and trust in

God was really being put to the test: this was the most desperate situation we had been in thus far. We were in agreement that we would not turn to friends or family to help us out but trust that God would rescue us and provide for us. This was not out of a sense of pride but a sense that we wanted to know that God was true to His word as we had been taught. Etched in my mind is my husband's concerned face as he went out the door to work that morning; with tears in his eyes he reminded me we had prayed and there was no more we could do apart from trust that God would provide!

Around 10 am the telephone rang. It was friends from a nearby town who said they needed to come over to Bedford to do some shopping and could they come round for lunch! Before I had time to gasp or faint from fear they chimed in announcing that they would bring something in from the fish shop for us all to eat! I put the phone down and immediately erupted in praise and thanksgiving - it looked like the little one and I would eat lunch. True to their word they came and brought us a lovely fish and chip lunch, after which they asked if I would go to town with them and help them to find items of school uniform they needed for one of their children. On getting into town they said they just needed to pop in to a supermarket to get a few bits; in the back of my mind I was thinking how God seemed to be having a joke on me - if only they knew how desperately we needed food.

Well it turned out that they did know! On entering the supermarket they thrust a trolley in my hands and told me to fill it with food, explaining to me that they had received a gift of money in the post that morning and had felt upon receiving it that it was meant to help someone else. So they had prayed and asked God to show them who it was and said that He had clearly told them that I had no food and to come and take me shopping!

What an amazing experience it was – I was just putting in the shopping trolley what I considered to be essentials and choosing the cheapest brands as they were removing them and replacing them with the best brands and piling in luxury items that I would never have afforded to buy for us.

What a sight greeted the older boys and my husband when they came in from school and work that night! The refrigerator was full of food, the freezer was packed full, as was the food cupboard. Fruit and food in abundance overflowed on the work surfaces. My husband's immediate response was 'I knew God would do it –how did He do it?' We were learning that Jehovah -Jireh is indeed our abundant provider!

On another occasion, one Sunday morning when we had run out of both money and food, having eaten the last of the food we had in the house for our breakfasts, we went to church as usual.

After the service a friend was chatting to me and in the course of a general conversation asked me what we were having for Sunday lunch. My response was 'I don't know yet,' for sure I didn't – it wasn't a lie. Having prayed about it, I was waiting for God to provide. My friend then challenged me, 'The truth is that you haven't got food have you? God has told me to take you home with me and fill a bag of food for you.' This lady was a relatively new Christian and was so encouraged to find out that she had heard God correctly and I was so encouraged that once again God had provided so I could feed my family. The food that she gave me lasted us for two days until we received a payment that was due to us, when we were able to stock up the larder again.

I also recall one Christmas time when Father God totally amazed me in His generous provision for us. One day just before Christmas I was standing in a queue in M & S waiting to pay for some small item that I had bought when I noticed the shopping basket belonging to the lady in front of me. It was laden with festive goodies. I looked and thought how lovely it must be to be able to afford such luxuries for Christmas and that was it, I thought no more about it. I am sure you can imagine my amazement when a day or so later my husband came home with a Christmas gift from work – a M & S Christmas Hamper – everything I had seen in the lady's basket and more!

This was a lesson to me about how Father God not only provides but that He watches over us - even our thought life and how He loves to surprise and bless us with the unspoken desires of our heart.

Chapter 11

Ryvita Meal

There was one particular time when we were desperately low on food that initially God appeared to have let us down. It was a Saturday morning and we had used what money we had to enable us to go to an FGB breakfast meeting. I went to the meeting with the thought in mind, 'I will think about what we will have for lunch later.' There was a guest speaker who had travelled from London, who shared with us about his own journey of faith with God. In the midst of his talk I heard God say to me 'Invite him back for lunch' then pursued a dialogue with God about how we didn't have anything to feed him for lunch! I managed to beckon to my husband who was seated on the top table with the speaker and whispered in his ear what I felt God was saying to me and said how God seemed insistent that we cannot send this man back to London without feeding him. My husband, being fully aware of the food situation at home, spoke to all the other officers who were there and tactfully asked if any of them were able to take the speaker back home and provide him lunch. All of them said they couldn't as they already had plans in place for later in the day.

So it seemed it was down to us, once again being dependent upon God's provision. My husband suggested that I travel back home with the speaker and he would follow on. At the time I was none too pleased about this wondering why he didn't travel with the man. It was only later that I found out that my husband had scooted round to see someone who owed us money in the hope of getting it and enabling him to quickly buy some food but God had other plans!

As I travelled home with the speaker he was still in speaker mode and was overflowing with how he had learnt the importance of living by faith. I sat there quietly thinking to myself 'I hope he believes all he is saying because his faith is just about to be put to the test.' I was hoping and praying that when we got home I would find that a bag of food had been delivered or left on the doorstep, this was not to be the case. As I welcomed him in to our home I explained that we lived a very modest life-style but that we couldn't send him back to London without offering him some lunch. I ushered him in to the lounge and left him to chat with a girl who was staying with us at the time following the breakdown of her marriage. I then dived into the toilet and got down on my knees and cried out to God 'what shall I give him? Back came the reply, 'Give him what you've got!' I could scarcely believe my ears; God had always up to this point provided abundantly but now He was saying to use what we had, which was next to nothing! I checked out that I had heard Him right and again came 'Give him what you've got,' only this time along with the words came an overwhelming sense of supernatural peace that enabled me to rise from my knees and confidently go and prepare lunch with what little food we had. The children were all out for the day and taken care of, so I just had to scrape something together for the four of us.

All I had was a few *Ryvita's* which I put on a plate, the smallest amount of spread that I put on a saucer trying to make it look as though there was more than there actually was, and a jar of peanut butter and some Marmite. In a cake tin I had a chocolate birthday cake all decorated with candles on top that I had made to celebrate a friend's birthday later in the day. I thought, 'Needs must! Our friend will have to sacrifice his birthday cake.' So I whipped out all the candles and cut it up in to slices, the only problem was, it then looked like a worm had made holes in it where the candle- holders had been! We had tea bags and milk so I was able to make a pot of tea to go with the banquet and laid it all out on the dining table making it look as appetising as I possibly could.

During that lunch I experienced something I had never experienced before or since. After eating only a couple of Ryvita's I felt really full as though I had eaten a big meal. I sat there quietly marvelling to myself at this phenomenon and fervently praying that our guest was having the same experience.

After lunch, as our guest got up to leave and we were saying our goodbyes, he quietly said 'I think I am just learning what faith is all about.' Within a couple of hours of his departure God brought a friend with a bag of food that lasted us several days until we received our next pay cheque. I really could not understand God's timing in all this, however a few weeks later all became clear.

We saw advertised that the speaker was part of an Evangelistic team ministering at a local church outreach event, so we decided to go along.

Upon recognising us he took us aside to speak to us privately and explained to us how God had used our hospitality and the Ryvita meal to speak to him profoundly. He told us that following a change in his work he had taken a substantial wage cut and yet had continued to live a luxurious life-style, living way beyond his means until he had stacked up an enormous overdraft. God had used the modest meal I had provided to open his eyes to the fact he needed to cut according to the cloth and bring him to a place of repentance. All glory to Jesus!

Our hearts overflowed with joy as we listened to the work God had done in this man's life through our simple obedience in giving him what we had! We were further blessed when he presented us with a massive homemade steak pie that his wife had lovingly made for us. What a lesson this was for us in being obedient to what God says and trusting Him even when we do not understand what He is doing.

I can definitely vouch that obedience brings blessing. Within two weeks of the Ryvita meal we had paid off all our debts and had cash flow and food.

Point to ponder: It may be that you are struggling in today's financial climate. Why not chat to God about your needs and ask Him to provide?

Chapter 12

Give and it will be Given unto You

Another irrational act of obedience to God's prompting that brought us abundance of blessing was one day when I was chatting to a neighbour who had recently come to faith and was financially in a no better place than us. She happened to comment how much she liked the skirt I always wore to church on Sundays. Without thinking about it I told her she could have it and gave it to her. When I came home reality hit that actually I had given my only skirt away! I had no doubt at all that God had wanted me to bless her with it, but now I was faced with the problem of not having a Sunday outfit myself. It looked like it would have to be jeans!

A couple of days later on a Saturday, a friend from London came to visit and told me that she had cleaned out her wardrobe and asked if I would be offended to accept the bags of clothes she had brought thinking that I might like them. Of course I wasn't offended and was hoping that there might be a skirt amongst in there somewhere.

Well hope did not disappoint! There wasn't just one skirt – there were several skirts; really nice ones as well as lots of other lovely items of clothing. There was so much that I gave some away and blessed other people. Quite unwittingly I seemed to have unlocked Kingdom truth: Luke 6:38 says 'Give and it will be given unto you' … from that point on, for some considerable time, clothes kept pouring in to us. I was given beautiful designer outfits that were beyond my wildest dreams of owning, my husband was given expensive suits and shirts all of which fitted him. This in itself was amazing as my husband was not standard size, being tall with a broad build. It really was quite an enigma as clothes were pouring in almost on a daily basis and as fast as I gave them away more would come in. Yet at the same time we were still praying-in finances and food.

I recall one night feeling totally frustrated, I went round to see a friend and with tears I poured out my frustrations to her. 'What is God doing? Does He think we can eat clothes?' After a cup of tea and a chat she walked back home with me. When we walked in the house there on the settee were two bags of clothes that someone had brought round whilst I had been out! We just burst out laughing! Eventually the flow of clothing stopped and finances improved but when I think back I do still wonder what the clothes were all about. Maybe we should have sold them? I don't think so! God loves to bless and is a generous giver of good things.

Chapter 13

Increased Faith

God has certainly surprised me at times in some of the ways that He has blessed me. One such time was the first National Conference of Aglow that I went to.

The first night I was there I had a dream that I was sharing with someone how God had supplied us with £50 and then £500 and how God had spoken to me and said to me 'There is plenty more where that came from, you haven't seen anything yet!'

The following day I could hardly believe my ears when the National President threw out a challenge as to who would believe God to provide a way for them to go to the World Aglow conference to be held later in the year at Niagara Falls in Buffalo, New York State. Not only had I had the dream the night before but I suddenly recalled the day before I had gone to the conference I was doing some shopping in town and found myself looking in a shop window at a set of suitcases and the thought had passed through my mind, 'I wonder what it would be like to own a set of suitcases like that and fly off to America.' My heart and mind was racing at the thought that God could possibly be calling me to go and would challenge my faith with something as big as this.

The following night I didn't dream, as I hardly slept at all. My bedroom was situated near the water tank of the house and all night there was a constant drip, drip of water and with it the word 'Niagara' kept swirling in my mind. I knew in my heart God was confirming to me that He was calling me to go but I couldn't see how it would be possible either financially or because of family responsibilities. I began to wonder what on earth my husband would think when I returned home from the conference and shared with him. His response was amazing! Ever the generous, kind hearted, practical man of faith, he said 'If God is calling you to go, you must go and we will know for sure if He is, as He will have to provide.'

This was the biggest faith challenge to us up to that point. As we prayed and discussed it, I confessed I really didn't feel I had the faith to believe for the whole amount in one go to cover conference fees, hotel and flights; so we came to a place of agreement that we would start small and ask God to provide money for me to get a passport.

A few weeks went by when one morning I received a letter with £20 in it from my sister in Australia, she had never done anything like this before and I have to confess I was a little slow on the uptake. I was so thrilled that she had sent money for me to spend on myself that I was looking what I could treat myself to when God reminded me and made it clear to me that this was His provision to get a passport. This greatly encouraged us in our faith that God indeed would provide. We pressed on praying for God to provide bit by bit for us as it was needed, and He did not let us down. At every deadline along the way He provided for conference fees, hotel and flight costs; sometimes it was the eleventh hour and our faith was put to the test, but it came! Faithful friends rallied round us and stood in faith with us and offered to take care of the family whilst I was away. So it was that I followed God's call and found myself sitting on a plane flying to the USA.

Chapter 14

A Faith Challenge

I find it difficult to find words that adequately describe my feelings and emotions when I sat there on the plane with tears of joy and awe trickling down my cheeks, as I read a book about Smith-Wigglesworth and some of his adventures of faith and here I was having my own little adventure of faith. The lady sitting next to me must have thought the tears were due to fear and asked if it was the first time I had flown, enquiring if I was nervous. I explained that I was flying out to a Christian conference and how I was in a total state of awe because of the amazing ways in which God had provided for me, making it possible for me to go.

At the time the whole experience seemed totally surreal to me. Here I was sitting on a plane going to America when the furthest I had ever travelled before was to the Isle of Wight. I think I was too awestruck to be nervous!

As the power of the engines roared, thrusting the plane up high in to the sky, I was overwhelmed with gratitude to God my Father for the blessings He was pouring out up on my life and I sat there silently giving Him praise and adoration for His goodness towards me.

There seemed to be such a correlation between what I was experiencing in the physical sense and in the spiritual sense. I thought of how the power from the engines of the plane had lifted us up above the clouds giving me an experience that I would never have dreamt of having. I could not help but think of how my life had so dramatically changed since deciding to accept Jesus as my

Saviour and Lord and how the power of the Holy Spirit at work in my life was taking me to new heights, new places and giving me new experiences beyond my wildest dreams or expectations.

I had an amazing time at the conference listening to testimonies and faith-building teaching and was so blessed by the worship. It was the first time I had experienced worshipping and Praising God with thousands of other like-minded women; there was such an incredible sense of God's presence in the building. For sure it felt like Heaven touching earth!

As if to keep me earthed a bit, to be sure God gave me a faith challenge. In one of the sessions early on in the conference there was an offering being taken and we were requested to ask God the amount He would have us put in. So I asked and felt Him ask me to put in all I had in my purse! This was all I had for spending money to last me throughout the trip - this was definitely one of those times when I questioned whether I was hearing God's voice. Somehow my faith rose to trust that God knew what I needed and I emptied out my purse into the offering basket. After the session someone came up to me and said my name was on the notice board requesting me to go to the information desk. When I went I was told that there had been an error in my registration fees and I had overpaid and was due a refund. The refund turned out to be more than I had put in the offering! How good is our God?

Apart from attending the conference I also enjoyed making new friends and learning a bit more about the American way of life. I did suffer one rather embarrassing experience; I found myself the centre of attention one day as I tried to cross a road and a policeman yelled through a megaphone at me and told me off for jay walking. I didn't do that again!

During a free period from the conference some of us went on an excursion to see Niagara Falls and the Robert Moses Power Plant. Niagara Falls truly is one of the greatest natural wonders of the world, a demonstration of the awesome power and beauty of our creator God. The sheer power force and roar of the water is quite breath taking. The noise of the rushing waters was thunderous, I wondered if it sounded like the voice the Apostle John referred to in Revelation when he described the voice of someone being like the son of man 'Whose voice was like the sound of rushing waters.'

It was whilst we were doing a tour of the Robert Moses Power Plant that I felt God speaking to my heart and giving me revelation. A guide explained how water is diverted from the Niagara River and up to 375,000 gallons a second flows through the plant's turbines and that then powers generators which convert mechanical energy into electrical energy. It is the biggest supplier of clean carbon-free hydro-electricity in New York State, bringing light and power to thousands of homes and industries in the surrounding area.

Whilst listening to the guide I had a powerful sense of God's presence and Him showing me a spiritual parallel. How through putting my faith in Him, I had been converted into newness of life , been given the power of the Holy Spirit and commissioned to bring the light and power of the gospel to those around me. Moses power plant is one of the places where I will always remember God affirming a call on my life to serve Him. I returned home with renewed zeal and passion to light up the world for Jesus!

Chapter 15

How Lovely is Your Dwelling Place

> Psalm 84 verses 1-2
> How lovely is your dwelling place O Lord of Hosts, my soul faints and yearns for Your courts.

My parents were thrilled to see how my faith was growing and had been as amazed as I was, in the way that God had provided for me to go to the conference in the USA. Neither of them ever having travelled abroad themselves, on my return they were eager to hear all the exciting news about the trip. I knew the thing that really overjoyed them was that after years of praying for me and believing that one day I would come back to God, they had lived to see it come to pass and was now able to enjoy watching God work His purposes out in my life.

After all the years I had spent kicking my heels and rebelling against God and my parents, I now had a new relationship with them that was firmly rooted in our shared faith and love for Jesus.

During the summer months following my trip to the States my mother complained of feeling totally exhausted which was not like her at all and asked if they could come and stay with us for a few days. My husband had holiday due so he took a couple of weeks off work and fetched them to stay with us. We had a lovely two weeks holiday with them, the weather was good and we were able to take them out and about for day trips. I had noticed that my mother didn't seem to have much of an appetite, although she seemed cheerful enough and enjoyed seeing and spoiling the grandchildren, so I wasn't too concerned. However the day before we were due to take them home she came out in a rash and was in a lot of pain, we had to get the doctor out who diagnosed she had a bad case of shingles; so it was that they stayed on with us for another six weeks until she was recovered enough for them to return home again.

Now looking back I see those six weeks as a real gift from Father God. As you may recall call from earlier chapters I hadn't had a particularly close relationship emotionally with my mother when I was a child. However during the six weeks of her convalescence I felt a new bonding and understanding of each other taking place in our mother and daughter relationship, and of course an added blessing for us both was that we were now sisters in the Lord as well!

I began to see my mother's faith from a new perspective. Although to my knowledge my maternal grandparents weren't Christians they sent their children, including my mother, to the Anglican Sunday School that was held in the village. When she was fourteen she heard about a Bible study group that was held in the village Baptist chapel and started to attend that as well as going to Sunday School. Somewhere along the way between the two, she came to find a place of personal faith in God and decided to declare her commitment to Him by being confirmed in the Anglican Church, although she still kept attending the Baptist chapel.

It was at the Bible study group where she met my father and they began dating (or courting as the term was back then) when they were both fourteen.

On leaving school my mother left home and the village to live with an aunt in Nottingham, where she worked in service as a nanny, caring for a little boy. Despite distance between them, my parents kept their romance alive via letters and holiday visits until at twenty - one years of age she returned to the village to marry my father.

During our chats she told me how getting married for her was not an easy decision. Although they were deeply in love she felt that in marrying my father and making a commitment to him that she also needed to be committed to the Baptist church where he was training to be a lay preacher. So it was after much thoughtful consideration that she sacrificed her love of the Anglican liturgy and way of doing church, and out of love for my father she entered marriage fully supporting his dedication and calling to serve God within the Baptist denomination.

She shared with me how baptism by total immersion, a fundamental requirement to Baptist doctrine, had given her some problems. Not that she didn't believe in it, but in her eyes the vows she had made to God at her confirmation had been sacred to her and sufficient. Whilst my father never put any pressure on her to be baptised apparently through the years there were some people that did; this had caused her pain and sadness in that she felt her faith wasn't being accepted as real and at times had fought against feelings of being a second class Christian.

She described to me how much she enjoyed the latter years of married life after father had retired when they had time to sit and pray and read the Bible together. This was the time when she felt she had her husband to herself, without the demands of a busy life and could ask him all the biblical questions she had stored up through the years.

By the time my parents returned home I felt the relationship between my mother and me was the strongest I had ever known. Within a month of them returning home I received a phone call from my mother to say that a large strawberry coloured lump had appeared on her neck and she had been to see her GP who had referred her to hospital and had suggested that she take someone with her to the appointment, so would I go with her. I went home immediately, and on seeing see a consultant at the hospital we were told that she had cancer, that it was serious and that she would need to be cared for.

I was quite shocked as she looked physically well; it was my father who suffered from Parkinson's disease and who appeared to be the frail one. Plans had to be put in place quickly: it was my mother's wish to come and live with us, to which my husband and I agreed would be the best plan. Somehow we would find room for them to move in with us and we would care for them. So over the next few days while he worked on caring for the boys and changing things around in our home, converting the lounge/dining room in to a bed-sitting room I stayed with my parents and helped them pack up their essential belongings for the move.

One of the first things we had to do after moving them in with us was register them with our GP practice and get my mother's medical notes transferred so she could see a consultant at our local hospital. We were fast-tracked for her to see a consultant who after giving her a thorough examination, took me aside and told me that she had cancer throughout her body and that her time left on earth was short. His estimated time was six weeks. He offered to admit her in to hospital to be cared for; I refused this as an option and said I would take her home to be cared for by her family.

After having everything explained to her I brought her home; I was reeling in shock at the news we had received but also in awe at my mother's peace and composure. Many people commented on her calm and assured faith in God that shone from her like a brilliant light shining in the darkness. Her response to the news was a call to action, if there was little time left she wanted the family home emptied and sent me on a mission to do it! What amazed me was she could tell me where every single thing was; what was in certain cupboards and drawers, who I was to give what to, all down to the last detail, so it was all done in next to no time with great simplicity. I knew she had good organisational skills but this all seemed to be too organised and I asked her if she had known that she would need to do this; it was then she told me for several months she had woken up in the night and found herself singing the hymn 'Abide with me, fast falls the eventide' and had felt such a strong sense of God's presence and had sensed that He was preparing her for eternity, that her time was nearing to leave this earth and be with Him forever.

Having got my parents settled in to our home it was hard to believe the prognosis she had been given. District nurses were popping in and checking up on how she was doing and were surprised that she was so bright, peaceful and pain free apart from what she described as mild discomfort. Indeed the Consultant at the hospital had been accurate with his assessment of time, we were given exactly six precious weeks together; most of which was enjoying quality mother and daughter time. She was up and about helping with simple chores like drying the dishes, I would wash and set her hair and cook appetising food or whatever she fancied. We paid for someone to come in and do the main housework so freeing me up to spend as much time as possible with her. It was only the last few days when she became so physically weak that she took to her bed. One time after my husband had lifted her in and out of bed she said to me how thankful to God she was that He had blessed her with me, a daughter to care for her and a son as well; and how when I was born she hadn't understood God and thought that He hadn't answered her prayer, but could now see that He had given her so much more.

I so value the love and prayer support given to us at that time by family and friends and the strength God gave us sustaining us through His word. It was reported back to us some time later by one of the nurses who had been a regular in our home that some of the other nurses after visiting us would comment on the peace they experienced and were taken aback by the amount of Bibles they saw dotted around the house that all seemed to be read.

One day as she lay in bed I had the idea of asking her if she would like me to ask an Anglican Vicar to come and pray with her. Immediately her eyes lit up and she responded with how much she would like that. So I contacted one who I knew well as he served as an advisor for us in Women's

Aglow. I recall the night he came round so vividly, a friend was visiting and we sat down one end of the room with my husband while he sat at the other end with my father at my mother's bedside and prayed some liturgical prayers and read from the Bible. The whole room was filled with God's presence; it was the most amazing experience, as though we were on privileged Holy ground. It felt as though we were witnessing something that was too sacred to be shared, as a final desire of her heart was fulfilled.

It was on a Sunday evening a couple of days after this, that I sat holding her hand as her life neared its end. I thought about how much I loved her and what a privilege it had been to care for her and to have this time with her and I realised how much of her life had been spent bringing the light and power of the gospel through the love and compassion of Jesus that flowed through her to the many people she cared for throughout the years.

As she took her final breaths I had a picture of a man in a long gown holding the hand of a young woman walking away from me up a green hillside and I knew she was gone from me and safe forever with her Lord! Through tears of loss and sadness I knelt down and sang a song of worship based on Psalm 84 'How lovely is your dwelling place O Lord of Hosts, my soul faints and yearns for your courts.'

My mum was home!

Point to ponder: Where is home to you? Do you have an assurance that you have a home in Heaven?

Chapter 16

God my Sufficiency

2 Corinthians 12 verse 9
My grace is sufficient for you, for My power is made perfect in weakness.

There are times in life when you think things couldn't possibly get any worse - then they do!

To make things easier for us the evening my mum went home to be with the Lord our lovely neighbours had taken our youngest son, who was then aged six, to have a sleep-over next door. During the night he had been sick and crying with stomach pains, after calling the GP out in the morning he was admitted to hospital and operated on for appendicitis.

Within twenty-four hours of losing my mum, my baby was in hospital. I had a father grieving the loss of his wife and two other children grieving the loss of their grandmother, all needing my love and support. To be truthful much of that time is a fog to me; I have no recollection at all of registering my mother's death or making funeral arrangements. One thing I do recall is the loving care and support given us by friends and family who helped us in so many ways to get through those difficult days. Some of our church family helped out by taking shifts at the hospital to stay and play with our son as he recovered from surgery, enabling us to get some rest and give time and attention to the rest of the family. So much love was poured upon us in so many ways for which I was and still am and always will be, truly thankful - both to God and to them.

All this took place just three weeks before Christmas. With the funeral of my mum having taken place and our youngest home from hospital I was faced with the daunting prospect of preparing for my first Christmas without my mother. I did my best to make preparations through a veil of tears. I recall one day just sobbing in my husband's arms and feeling an overwhelming sense of loss and sadness and feeling like I never wanted to see another Christmas. What we did or how we spent that Christmas, I have no recollection at all!

It took me a good eighteen months to two years to regain emotional strength following all the traumatic events that had taken place over such a short space of time.

Initially I was so vulnerable to negative thoughts and had to fight fear over things like what effect my mother's death would have upon my father. They had been so close in their relationship I feared that I might soon lose him too.

As is often the case, I am pleased to say those particular fears and anxieties proved to be a waste of emotional energy; my father built himself a new life and lived happily with us for another ten years.

I was particularly blessed by a phone call I had from a sister in Christ who lived miles away and whom I barely knew; only having met her a couple of times at FGB meetings when her husband had been the guest speaker. They had heard that I had stepped down from leadership in Aglow due to the change in family circumstances and how I was emotionally exhausted following the death of my mother. This dear lady called me up and poured so much love down the phone, inviting me to go and stay with them so that I could be loved back to strength. That phone call always sticks in my mind, for although I never took them up on their offer, the words of kindness and love spoken to me over the phone brought me so much comfort; like balm on a wounded heart.

Another thing that brought me much comfort and I am sure sustained me through what I can only describe as a 'dark night of the soul' season, was God's Word - reading the Bible. A particular verse that someone sent me on a card at that time became like daily medicine to me, it was 2 Corinthians 12 verse 9 'My grace is sufficient for you, for my power is made perfect in weakness.' I clung on to it like a child would hang on to a comfort blanket. Now I can look back and say of that time and many other times too, that God is true to His word and indeed has been my sufficiency.

Chapter 17

A New Season

The downside of having American friends who were over here because their spouses were in the military is that they were eventually posted back to the USA and as I had grown close to several of them, it was quite a loss to me. It was the end of a season that had been rich in friendship and spiritual growth for us all.

I have always been amazed at how God brings the right people in to our lives at just the right time. The ladies on the airbase had been a real strength to me when I had most needed it. Now it was time for us all to move on in to a new season.

One evening some friends, a Pastor and his wife, invited us over for a meal wanting to introduce us to a couple who had recently got married and had moved in to the area where we live. She was American and he was English and they had met through a mutual friend who was a missionary in Brazil. They were a lovely friendly couple who we quickly found out had a sense of humour when my husband knocked over a glass of lemonade that went all over the poor girl!

Little did I know that night that God had connected me with another American sister who would become a faithful friend and prayer partner for several years to come. We were united by a common passion in our love for God and desire to grow and walk in His ways; we met almost on a daily basis for fellowship, when we would study the Bible, pray together and share about whatever was going on in our lives at that particular time. Actually it was amazing the things we had in common: we had both grown up in quite strict Christian homes of Baptist background and we both had been encouraged and inspired to grow in our faith by aunts who were passionate in their love for Jesus.

For a time we did new testament style church and met together in our home on Sunday afternoons, reaching out to some of the children in the local area. It was a golden opportunity for our youngest son to invite some of his friends along to have some fun learning biblical truths and hearing about the love of Jesus.

It came as quite as surprise to us when one day we shared with each other how we felt God was speaking to us about attending the local Anglican Church. The fact that we had both individually heard the same thing caused us to investigate further what we felt to be God's promptings, so one Sunday we went along to a morning service.

It was quite amazing because the liturgical service was so foreign to us yet we felt quite at home and had a quiet assurance within us that this is where God wanted us to be. Also unbeknown to us was at the exact same time a new Priest had been appointed to lead the church.

Although the services were totally different from anything I had been used to in my Baptist upbringing I soon settled in and quickly grew to love some of the Anglican liturgy and as part of my commitment to God's calling to be part of the church I was duly confirmed.

My friend soon got involved with the children's work and I tended to focus on pastoral work -in particular visiting and caring for the sick and infirm. I found the Priest to be very supportive and compassionate towards people God brought across my path to care for.

Margaret was the mother of two boys, one of whom had been a friend all through school with our middle son. Tragedy had hit their family when the father was fatally injured through an accident at work when the youngest boy was about six years old. This was around the time when I had first come back to faith; when I heard about the accident and Margaret's husband being in the intensive care unit fighting for his life I went round to see her full of faith assuring her that people were praying and believing her husband would be healed. After he had died I went round to see her and cried with her sharing her sorrow and was at a loss for words of explanation as to how God could have let this happen. She was such a gracious woman who didn't speak about faith and neither did she pass judgement on me regarding what seemed to be the false hope I had given her and from this point a lasting friendship was formed between us.

It was ten years later when she herself was diagnosed with cancer of the mouth which proved to be terminal, that our friendship deepened and as a family we had the privilege of caring for her and thus demonstrating the love and compassion of Jesus. The faithfulness of God was just amazing through those times. I recall my husband revising for some exams while sitting in the visitors' lounge at the hospital whilst I sat with her when she was enduring gruelling treatment. He passed the exams with flying colours! When she was no longer able to cope at home we had her come and stay with us where she was able to come with me on speaking engagements when she was up to it and just enjoy being cared for.

Although my father was living with us, by now our eldest son had left home so we had a spare bedroom in which we could accommodate her until such a time when she needed palliative care so went into the local hospice.

Throughout this emotional journey I found the Priest to be an incredible spiritual and practical support: he came with me to team meetings about her level of care and was a very real strength for her and her boys, right to the end.

Another twist in how God brings people together is when my friend was staying with us she had a new social worker assigned to her who turned out to be a Christian. We became good friends and in due course my husband was best man for him when he got married.

Chapter 18

Jean

I first met Jean soon after I came back to faith when her daughter, who was a close neighbour and who worked full time, asked me if I would mind popping in to see her mother at lunch times to check that she was OK. She explained to me that her father was at work in the daytime and that her mother, who had a history of depression and also suffered from angina, was confined to bed after taking several falls in the home.

It was these lunchtime visits when I would fix her some lunch and spend a bit of time with her that became the foundation of a close friendship that spanned thirty odd years until at a ripe old age; she went home to be with the Lord.

When I first met her she was a pitiful sight, bless her, black and blue with bruises and grazes from where she had fallen. Unfortunately it was a sight that would greet me many times after that and eventually led to her husband taking early retirement to care for her. After several years and many medical opinions she was finally diagnosed as having some kind of epilepsy and was then put on medication that controlled it.

From the beginning I was open about my faith and let her know that she was in my prayers. I explained to her how reading the scriptures brought me comfort and strength and when I asked if I could read some to her, she welcomed the idea. I was never sure in those early days if she understood anything of what I read to her but for sure I witnessed God bringing peace to her spirit as I read.

After her husband took retirement to care for her my visits were less frequent. I would pop in occasionally and see how they were both doing and was always pleased to see her up and hear reports that there had been no angina attacks or falls.

On one of my random visits her husband greeted me with such a forlorn expression on his face. On enquiring whatever could be wrong he told me things had been going so well for them regarding Jean's health, that they had booked to go on holiday and were due to go the next day.

There was Jean lying on the settee suffering from a severe angina attack and he was on the verge of cancelling the holiday. I felt overwhelmed with a deep compassion for this lovely couple, declared that they would go on holiday and said I would pray that Jesus would heal her.

I held her hands and prayed in Jesus' Name that she be healed and that they would be able to go on holiday.

It was most strange because after I had prayed and left I never really thought about them or their holiday again until one day a few weeks later when I was out running with their daughter and she asked me if I had prayed with her mum before they went on holiday. Then it sprang back into my mind! 'What happened? How did it go?' I enquired. 'Well,' came back the response, 'They went on holiday and mum hasn't had an angina attack since!'

I have no doubt that the overwhelming compassion I felt that day when I prayed for her was the compassion of Christ, and all Glory to Him, she was indeed healed. A few months after that she was discharged from the cardiologist with a good report and to my knowledge never suffered another angina attack to her dying day.

After hearing the amazing report from her daughter I went round to visit her parents and hear the story first hand. They shared with me about the wonderful holiday they had had and how Jean had been in good health throughout. However what really struck me was the difference in Jean's demeanour: there was a new life sparkling in her eyes and a stream of questions regarding her healing that I couldn't answer. Indeed who can explain the sovereign acts of God and his wonderful deeds to mankind? One thing was very clear, she had had an encounter with Jesus Christ and from that time on she wanted to learn all she could about Him.

Romans 2 verse 4 talks about God's kindness or goodness leading to repentance; this was most certainly the case in Jean's life - her heart continually overflowed with love and thanksgiving to Jesus for setting her free from angina.

Jean asked me to buy her a Bible, which I did and she quickly developed a love of reading it and having it read to her. She started coming to church with me, making Christian friends and developing a love of Christian songs.

I don't recall ever praying the prayer of salvation with her, although I am quite sure at some point I did. It was such a joy and privilege to watch her grow in her love relationship with the Lord. Sometimes my American friend would go and visit her and take her guitar and minister to her in song and one of Jean's favourites was a song written by my friend called 'I'm married to Jesus – my bridegroom forever,' I think why it was one of her favourites was because it so expressed her new found heart of love for the Lord.

It is interesting that although God had healed her from angina, in the years following we prayed many times for her to be healed from the dark times of depression and from the episodes that we later found out to be epilepsy, yet she never was. All I can say regarding that, is that God was true to His Word (2 Corinthians 12 verse 9) and His grace truly was sufficient for her through all times, good and bad. Her love for the Lord never waned.

After a time Jean decided she wanted to publicly acknowledge her faith by being confirmed. Due to her frailty and dislike of masses of people the Priest arranged with the Bishop for her to be confirmed in her own home with just a few close friends there. It was indeed a special occasion and one I will never forget, thanks to my American friend. After the solemnities of the occasion were over there was buffet food and drinks that my friend was duly serving up. I heard the Bishop request a glass of sherry and when I turned round, to my horror, I saw she had poured him up a tumbler full of sherry! Whispering in her ear I asked her what on earth she was doing? She then told me being a teetotaller she had no clue about alcohol measures. Frantic silent prayers were sent up that the Bishop would not go home tipsy! It certainly was a joyous occasion!

Another amazing work of grace I saw God do in Jean's life was in regard to her fifty some odd years of smoking cigarettes. She knew it was no good for her health and yet never seemed to have the inclination to stop. That is 'til one day she was talking to me about how she wished she could put money in the collection at church and because her husband didn't really understand her newly found walk of faith she felt it right not to ask him for money. Then suddenly she said 'I know if I stop smoking I will have money for God,' and that was it - she quit smoking after all those years and never had a withdrawal symptom! I am sure God honoured her heart of love. In 1 Samuel 2 verse 30 God says 'Those who honour me I will honour.'

Our friendship deepened with the years. I think we had a deep understanding of each other because we were both introvert type of characters. I understood her enjoying her own company and times of solitude with God. We would share our ups and downs, laughter and tears and pray together for our families. Indeed we saw God grant us some amazing answers to prayer particularly in relation to God blessing her youngest daughter and my nephew's wife with children, both of whom had had prolonged problems in conceiving and being able to carry children.

Many times I was amazed by Jean's acute sensitivity in hearing God's voice. On several occasions she spoke prophetically into my life with complete accuracy without me saying a word about anything I was seeking God about or going through at the time. Such times were real faith builders for us both.

During the years of our friendship she was hospitalised several times with various things; sometimes she was so poorly and had such a desire to go home to be with the Lord I would sit up all night with her. At other times I would care for her at home. Each time she pulled through she wondered why God hadn't taken her home. To me it was obvious – He still had a purpose for her being here! Her prayers were needed here!

Sadly it was her husband who, after a short illness, was to be the first to die. Afterwards everyone was concerned for Jean's safety with no one there to care for her. She eventually agreed with everyone's wishes to go in to a residential home where she received twenty-four hour care and happily spent the last few years of her life. It was a joy to visit her and see her being pampered in her old age, with manicures and hairdos and to hear about all the social activities that she was enjoying and of course we would chat about Jesus. It was as if she had found a new lease of life.

When the end finally came I was there with her lovely daughters as my precious friend finally got what she longed for as she slipped away from us and went home to be with her Lord.

My life was so enriched through knowing both Jean and her husband. My husband and I had grown to love them both, as though they were our own parents.

God taught me so much through them both. I saw them walk through some dark and difficult days and witnessed through Jean's husband what it meant to honour your marriage vows and honour each other in sickness and in health. I honour the memory of them both and thank God for bringing them in to my life.

Point to ponder: Take a moment to think about special friendships you may have or have had and pause to give God thanks for them.

Chapter 19

Street Encounters

Luke 10 verse 1

After this the Lord appointed seventy-two others and sent them two by two ahead of Him to every town and place where He was about to go.

Sometime after we started attending the Anglican Church the Priest suggested I should think about leading a group for a Lent course that was to be run. I was quite apprehensive about it but agreed that I would go along to the first training evening.

Whilst all the people there were lovely people, I felt quite out of my depth as I appeared to be the only person present who didn't come from an academic background. At the end of the meeting I made a hasty exit feeling somewhat overwhelmed and thinking this couldn't be something that God wanted me to do. However the Priest had other ideas: he followed me out in hot pursuit as I adamantly told him this was not for me, explaining that I felt like a fish out of water. His response, spoken with a loving authority, was that he saw me as brightly coloured fish very much in the water and in the water I would stay.

So it was, I completed the training and indeed went on to lead a Lent group and found I really enjoyed doing it. By the end of the six-week course we had formed friendships and enjoyed fun and fellowship together as we grappled with the questions the course presented to us. The outcome of that was that after the course had finished we continued to meet weekly as a house group. I led it for some time before handing over to someone else in the group, enabling them to develop their leadership skills. The group continued to run for well over twenty years and although the majority of the group are now quite aged with various infirmities they still visit each other and look out for each other. What a blessing!

I have often reflected through the years how this was a blessing that I could easily have missed out on had the Priest not challenged my insecurities when I initially tried to run away. In fact the eight years I spent under his ministry turned out to be quite cathartic. He had a knack of recognising potential and encouraging people to develop and use their gifting. I guess he saw potential and gifting within me that I had kind of locked away since stepping out of leadership in Aglow to care for my mother. Under his gentle guidance and affirmation I found hurts were gradually healed and my confidence restored and built upon.

I was really encouraged when the Priest asked if I would support him in introducing a less formal evening service once a month. I knew it came from a desire within him for us all to deepen in our walks with God through the empowering of the Holy Spirit and so agreed to journey with him on this venture.

I felt this was such a brave move on his part as there was great potential for people not to understand and want to stay in their comfort zones of Sunday evenings being about the traditional evensong services that they were accustomed to.

There were a few grumbles but nothing major and gradually we built up a support team as we explored as to what the services might look like. We gathered together a group of musicians to form a worship group. Well what a fun and interesting time that proved to be for me!

All of the musicians, apart from my American friend and a lovely young girl who was filled with the Holy Spirit and had a beautiful voice, were from traditional classical/choral background and were part of the formal church choir. They were truly lovely people however the modern songs we wanted to introduce came as a real culture shock to them. Initially there were quite a few protests and complaints that they would never be able to play such music as I was requesting.

Not being a musician myself I was very dependent upon God to show me how to get a breakthrough that would release these precious people in to a new sphere of worship. He did not let me down! I found out that two of the group who were struggling the most, actually played together in a jazz band and often did gigs together on Saturday nights. At the next rehearsal when they began to complain that they couldn't play what I was asking, I retorted with 'If they could joyfully play jazz together on a Saturday evening they could joyfully worship God with lively songs on a Sunday evening.' The result was amazing; it was as if making that declaration broke something off them. I am sure it wasn't insecurities that were holding them back as they were all very skilled musicians; more like the enemy of their souls who didn't want them to enhance their talents in giving praise to our glorious Lord!

It was amazing to witness the change in them. One of them, a lady who would have been in the forty -fifty age group, said she had always had a desire to learn to play the drums, so I encouraged her to go for it. To my utter amazement she did! She was so committed to learning and practising that she eventually became proficient enough to play the drums as part of the worship band in some of the services we did.

It was such fun encouraging people and watching them develop their talents and gifting whilst I too was developing mine. I enjoyed learning to plan and lead services and gained confidence in ministering the Word as the Priest gave me opportunity to preach at some of the services.

Sensing that God was calling me to some kind of ministry, I began to seek Him earnestly in prayer about the way I should go. At that present time I saw my main calling was to care for my father yet I also felt quite strongly that I should prepare for whatever God would have me do when I no longer had my father to care for. After sometime I shared my thoughts with the Priest and we began to pray and explore things together. This led me to doing some theological studies through distance learning with St. John's College, Nottingham, with the view to eventually training to become a Lay Reader in the Anglican Church.

This was definitely a season when life was far from boring. In fact I had some real fun times with God and witnessed some amazing things as I became obedient to His promptings.

A catalogue of amazing things happened after one street encounter I had with a gypsy lady I met when I was out walking with my American friend one morning. It was a nice sunny morning and my friend and I thought we would make the most of the sunshine and take her little boy out in his buggy for a walk. On route to her house I picked up a friend's toddler in her buggy and we set off chatting away as we enjoyed the beautiful spring morning when suddenly we were approached by a gypsy lady asking if I would buy some lucky lace or if she could tell my fortune. I responded with a sharply resounding 'No' and we proceeded to walk on and carried on with our chatting, when I suddenly stopped dead in my tracks as I felt the Holy Spirit convicting me of how rude I had been to the gypsy lady and that I should apologise to her. Leaving my friend to look after both buggies I ran back to speak to the gypsy who was now standing on someone's doorstep. Before I had chance to say anything to her a man opened the door and gave us both a sharp rebuff! I guess he thought he had a gypsy and a Jehovah's Witness knock his door at the same time!

With the door slammed in our faces I walked down the garden path with the gypsy and explained how I felt I needed to apologise to her for being rude and just snapping a 'No' at her without explaining myself. I went on to explain that I was a Christian and didn't believe in luck because I believe in God's blessing, at which point she told me she was a very sick woman and asked if I would pray for her. So there we were still standing on the path of the home where she had knocked on the door and I put my arm round her and simply prayed and asked God to heal her from the top of her head to the tip of her toes. It was then I remembered I had slipped in my pocket a little Christian card that I had received in the post just as I had been leaving the house that morning. It was a picture of the cross and read 'I asked Jesus how much He loved me and He held out His arms and died.' Wanting to bless her I handed the card to her, she responded by asking me if I would read it to her as she had never learnt to read. As I read it to her God was evidently touching her heart as I watched tears trickle down her cheeks. At the same time He was giving me more revelation and I picked up on if she had never learnt to read she probably didn't know what the Bible had to say about fortune telling. I explained in simple terms how it was offensive to God but that God loved her and wanted to bless her and asked if she had anything in her bag that she could sell that would earn her some money. She replied that she had some picture prints but no one ever bought them, so I asked her to do a deal with me and to quit the fortune telling and selling things to bring luck and trust that God would bless her and sell her pictures for her. Having found out during our conversation that her name was Bridget, I said goodbye to her and went back to join my friend who was anxiously waiting to hear what had gone on.

I really didn't expect to hear from Bridget again so imagine my surprise when several weeks later I was at the local shopping precinct chatting away to a friend, when the door of the chemist flew open and out ran Bridget running toward me with arms flailing repeatedly crying 'It's the woman of God! She didn't lie – God healed me!' She then proceeded to tell me how the morning I had met her in the street she was in so much pain with a gall bladder problem and had been told by the hospital that she would need surgery. She said she had been pain free from the time I had prayed for her and also that the same day she had sold every picture print that she'd had in her bag.

How awesome is God and how gracious of Him to let me know the outcome of that street encounter.

A few weeks after this on a hot summer day I was up town and decided to treat myself to an ice-cream from the ice-cream van. Who should be standing in the queue in front of me but Bridget! She then told the ice-cream man the story of how I had prayed for her and how God had healed her and instructed him to give me the biggest ice-cream he had as her treat to me.

Having bought the ice-cream she drew me aside and said how she believed God had brought me to the ice-cream van because she needed help and proceeded to tell me how her husband was violent towards her and kept beating her up and she would like me to go and visit her and maybe talk to him.

I enquired where she lived and found out she was living on a local gypsy site just outside of town, this particular site being infamous for violence and crime.

I needed wisdom and was not going to give her any quick answers or false hope so said I couldn't promise that I would go and visit her but I would promise to pray and ask God about it and if He so directed me then I would go.

On leaving town I went straight round to see my American friend and told her about the latest encounter with Bridget and asked her to pray also and seek God as to whether it was His will that we should visit Bridget at home, as I had no intention of visiting on my own. No wonder Jesus sent His disciples out two by two. After two or three days of waiting on God we both felt that although we were apprehensive about doing it, that indeed God would have us go and visit her.

It was about a week after meeting Bridget in town that my friend and I went to visit her. On making enquiries we found out which was her caravan and knocked the door. Bridget answered with a look of total amazement on her face saying how God had sent us just at the right time and went on to tell us that on the day she had met me in town, when she had arrived home her husband had beaten her up so badly that she ran away to get help from the police and that she had been staying in a safe house for a few days and that she had literally just returned home a few hours earlier. It transpired that her married son, who also lived on the same site was so angry with her for reporting his father in to the police, that he had tried to turn the caravan over with Bridget and her daughter in it, so she had once again called the police and said they had had only just left the site.

Welcoming us inside the caravan, Bridget said she was convinced that God had taken us at this time for me to talk some sense in to her son! My friend and I stared at each other in some trepidation and disbelief that this scenario was really happening to us.

I got down on my knees in the caravan and asked God for wisdom. Rising from my knees I said that I would go and speak to her son on two conditions: One; that her daughter would go with me and two; that she would pray with my friend for my protection whilst I was gone.

On agreement to my conditions I found myself being escorted by Bridget's daughter to the son's caravan. She knocked the door and without waiting for an answer, opened it for me to go in. Having stepped inside she closed the door behind me and shut me alone in the dimly lit caravan. As my eyes scanned down the caravan I suddenly locked eyes with a young couple who appeared to be naked sitting bolt upright in a double bed with the bed quilt pulled up to their chins, silently staring at me as if in disbelief. I really do not know who was in the biggest state of shock, them or me!

The silence was quickly broken as the young man shouted at me, 'You're the woman of God my mother told me about!' In that instant a mighty Holy Spirit anointing of boldness and authority came upon me as I confirmed indeed I was, I marched over to their bed and sat down and proceeded to give them a good dressing down as if they were my own children, regarding his shameful behaviour towards his mother. I explained to him how he needed to get things right with his mother and with God and how the Bible speaks clearly about honouring your father and your mother that things may go well with you all the days of your life. I told them about an evangelistic healing crusade that was going on in town that evening and said I would be there and that I expected to them to come along to it and to bring his mother as well. With that I turned on my heels and walked out of the caravan and reported back to Bridget and my friend about the conversation that had taken place. It was with great relief we said our goodbyes and walked off the site, both of us in total amazement at what we had just experienced of God's divine timings, leadings and protection.

That same evening I went to the crusade meeting in town with my husband. We had taken our seats when we saw Bridget walk in, led by her son, daughter, daughter-in law and several other young people who all went and sat at the very front of the church.

It was quite obviously a new and foreign experience to them as they sat chewing bubble gum and blowing the odd bubble with their gum. However they seemed to enter in and enjoy the exuberant Pentecostal worship and became totally transfixed and were nearly falling off their seats as they leaned forward and listened as a young man gave a testimony of how his life had miraculously changed since he had accepted Jesus Christ as his Saviour and told how God had transformed him and delivered him from living a life of crime and taking drugs into someone who now had found true purpose in life.

When an invitation was made for people to go forward if they wanted to receive Jesus as their Saviour the whole row of them jumped up and were the first ones to respond to the invitation.

Bridget herself received another healing from God. She had apparently been deaf in one of her ears and at the end of the service suddenly found she could hear perfectly well in both ears. God filled her to overflowing with the joy of the Holy Spirit. It truly was a sight to behold God doing a redeeming work in the whole family.

I often wonder what happened to Bridget and her family and pray the joy they found in the Lord that night has stayed with them.

Chapter 20

Years of Restoration

Joel 2 verse 25
I will repay you for the years the locusts have eaten ...

Following the death of my mother I was most concerned about how my father would adapt to life without her. They had always had such a close relationship; with his health being far from brilliant I had fears that it may not be long before he went to join her. However my fears proved to be unfounded and I was blessed and privileged to have him live on with us for another ten years.

I always look back on those ten years as a gift from my Heavenly Father repaying the years that the locusts had eaten (Joel 2 verse 25) in my case it was the years that had been lost with my earthly father, due to my own folly and rebellion throughout my teenage years and beyond. How good is God!

I held him as my hero of faith throughout the years; no matter what trials and tribulations came his way he always remained calm and steadfast in his faith and trust in God.

One day I asked him how he had coped and what he had thought when I was giving them so much grief and messing my life up when I was younger. Ever the joker he said, 'Well when you were a baby you were so cute I could have eaten you and when you were a teenager there were times when I wish I had done.' Then he came out with the usual words of Abrahamic faith and said he had dedicated me to God as a baby and he had every confidence that God would look after me and bring me back to Himself.

One of his favourite verses of Scripture was Isaiah 26 verse 3 'You will keep him in perfect peace, whose mind is steadfast because he trusts in you.' He certainly believed it and lived it out!
I was amazed one day when he told me how blessed he felt to see me so on fire for Jesus and being used by Him to reach people with His love and then said he almost felt envious of my testimony. He went on to explain how he never remembered a time when he didn't love Jesus. His earliest recollections were of sitting on his mother's knee as a small child and her singing hymns to him and reading Bible stories to him. His faith had grown stronger through the years and he had never wandered off the path so therefore felt he could not relate to people in the same way that I did because I had been in the world and tasted the pig's swill. Needless to say I would sooner have had his testimony. I would

have loved to have met my paternal grandmother, she sounded to be a lovely gracious woman of God but sadly she died two years before I was born.

It was such a blessing to share our walks of faith and witness the Holy Spirit at work in both of our lives. I recall one weekend when God brought about amazing forgiveness and restoration in our father/daughter relationship. It was a Saturday morning and I was in the kitchen baking cakes. As I stood at the kitchen table beating the cake mixture, I suddenly found myself weeping with a deep sense of sadness in my spirit. I realised it was something spiritual and feared that maybe God was about to take my father home to be with Him and this was His way of preparing me. The tears and sadness persisted all weekend, so much so I couldn't go to church on Sunday. I didn't say anything to my father and managed to hide from him how I was feeling. However on Monday morning I went down to see the Priest with box of tissues and Bible in hand and asked him to pray for me. As we prayed together he sensed that the sadness was indeed something to do with my father but not about him dying, but rather there was something I needed to forgive him for. He suggested I pray general prayers of forgiveness however I felt if there really was something specific then I needed to explore it with my dad and pray it through with him in person. The poor Priest was mortified at the thought of my dear old Dad being hurt and relationships fractured and agreed he would pray for me as I returned home to talk to him.

Imagine my surprise when I walked in to my dad's room and tentatively said I need to speak to him about something and his immediate response was 'First there is something I must speak to you about.' He then told me how he had been under the conviction of the Holy Spirit all weekend about the amount of time he had spent when I was a child doing things that he believed at the time to be God's work, preaching and being on several committees in the community that caused him so often to be out at meetings and he now realised how he had neglected my mother and me and he needed to ask my forgiveness! He was equally amazed when I told him about my weekend as we hugged and wept at God's awesome ways as I wholeheartedly forgave him.

Although Dad was frail in body with Parkinson's he was definitely strong in spirit and although he missed my mum terribly he had such a positive outlook that enabled him to settle in to a new way of life and I would say ministry.

He regularly attended two churches that arranged lifts for him; on Sunday mornings he went to a large church in town and on Sunday evenings he went to a small chapel in a nearby village and was very much committed in prayer and attendance to both.

He had such a multi-faceted ministry of encouragement that was greatly appreciated by many, visiting the housebound, befriending people in the street and was always writing letters of encouragement to people and brightening up people's lives with his sense of humour. The result of this was that he developed a massive circle of friends, who in turn would visit him or write to him at times when he wasn't well himself. One visit that stands out in my memory is of one time when he wasn't well when a Pentecostal Pastor and his wife came to visit him and pray for him. He had become friends with them after meeting and chatting to the Pastor's wife on a bus journey into town one day. As we prayed together I was struck by the spiritual growth that had taken place in Dad's latter years, he was so at ease with them praying in tongues, something that at one time would never have been acceptable, yet now was swallowed up in unity and an outpouring of God's love.

During the ten years he was with us he was diagnosed with several ailments: age-related diabetes, skin cancer and prostate cancer so hospital appointments became a familiar feature in our schedule. He was diagnosed with prostate cancer when he was eighty and once again I feared the worse. I remember sitting down with my Bible and pouring out all my fears and concerns to God and was led to read John 11. The words of verse four just leapt off the page in to my heart 'This sickness is not unto death; it is for the glory of God ... ' Peace flooded my heart and God fulfilled His word as Dad lived another six years after that diagnosis and prostate cancer was not the cause of his eventual death.

His final illness began as an arterial embolism which hospitalised him. I was with him when the consultant came to see us and explained that the anti-coagulant treatment was not working and in order to save his life they needed to amputate his leg. His immediate response was 'No.' The doctor, thinking he hadn't understood the seriousness, explained further that there was no blood supply getting to his leg and unless they did an amputation, gangrene would set in and that would certainly lead to death.

I sat at his bedside astounded at his response. He told the doctor that he understood perfectly well and that we all have to die sometime, that he had no fear of death and that he knew where he was going when he died and threw a gospel challenge back to the doctor! Eventually paperwork was put in place for my dad to sign to say that he had refused medical advice and had requested that I be allowed to bring him home to die. His wishes were granted, we were loaned a hospital bed on which to nurse him and, with the help of the district nurse team and the loyal support of friends, we were able to care for him at home right up to the end of his life here on earth.

I found the final weeks of Dad's life very difficult to bear emotionally. It was hard to see him in so much physical pain. How hard it is to watch our loved ones suffer! Yet as in every difficult situation prior and since – God's grace was my sufficiency!

My father had lived a long and blessed life and had seen the birth of three great-grandchildren. He was a true gentleman whose life demonstrated what it is to walk humbly with your God. (Micah 6 verse 8)

Thank you Jesus for my dad and the rich spiritual inheritance he left me!

Point to ponder: Maybe you are going through a difficult situation at the present time. My prayer for you is that God's grace will be your sufficiency, as it was mine.

Chapter 21

Dreams Come True

John 15 verse 7

If you remain in Me and My words remain in you, ask whatever you wish and it will be given you.

What I omitted to say in the previous chapter was that whilst caring for my father at the end of his life I was battling with my own physical health. It was around the very time his embolism problem occurred that I went to see the GP because I was feeling somewhat under par. By no means was I expecting to be told that I was suffering from fibroids and needed to be referred immediately for a hysterectomy.

I made the decision not to tell my father, as I knew it would bring back memories of all the pain and anguish he went through watching my sister's sufferings before she lost her battle against cancer. My focus was entirely on how I was going to care for Dad and how I could protect him from needless fear and distress.

I had asked my GP to refer me to a major teaching hospital that was in a nearby town and was surprised when I had an appointment come through within a couple of weeks to see a consultant. On examining me he confirmed the diagnosis of my GP and said I was to be booked in for immediate surgery. My response was this was not going to happen! I explained that I had cared for my father for the last ten years and was now nursing him through a terminal illness and that I had no intention of bailing out on him at this point in time!

Understanding the plight I was in, I was then asked if I would be willing to go on a drug research trial for six months with a fixed date for surgery in six month's time. The trial was to monitor the effectiveness of the drug in regards to it shrinking or breaking up the fibroids and I was told I would need to see the consultant on a monthly basis and have regular scans and check-ups and would be able to contact them any time with any concerns that I might have.

I gratefully accepted the offer, as I knew this was an answer to my prayers and the prayers of my faithful friends who were standing with me as I grappled to come to terms once again with all life seemed to be throwing at me.

From signing up for it, the drug programme gave me four weeks of precious time that I needed to look after my dad to the end of his life. As I said in the last chapter, God's grace was truly my sufficiency. I could see His loving hand of care in every step I took.

Through the drug programme I was not only given the precious gift of time I so desire or wished to have with Dad, but also the most excellent emotional support and medical care imaginable. I saw the same consultant each month when I would have check-ups and scans to see if the drugs were doing the job of shrinking the fibroids and indeed they were.

The five months between my father going home to be with the Lord and my surgery were quite surreal. I couldn't describe them as a roller coaster ride as they seemed to be one long plateau of coping and doing what needed to be done. Hospital appointments, making funeral arrangements, the funeral, my father's estate to sort out, his personal belongings to sort out and turning his bed-sitting room back in to a dining room all gave me little time to think about my forthcoming surgery. Neither did it give me time to grieve or process my loss.

It was as though my Heavenly Father held my hand every step of the journey!

The date for me to go in for my surgery just seemed to suddenly arrive although I had been aware of it for six months and I was filled with trepidation at the thought of major surgery and what it would entail. My faithful American friend and prayer partner took me into hospital and saw me settled in the ward and only left when she saw medics approaching! Herself having a dislike, if not fear, of needles, much to my amusement she decided that this was a good time for her to exit.

After she left I recall feeling quite alone and afraid when the Holy Spirit brought back to my mind an old hymn my grandfather used to sing 'I need thee, Oh I need thee, every hour I need thee; Oh, bless me now my Saviour, I come to thee.' What sustaining power I found through constantly releasing my fears to God as I soaked my mind in the words of that song.

I certainly felt blessed and encouraged when the anaesthetist came to see me and explained to me his role in looking after me during my surgery that was scheduled for the next day. As he was talking I noticed he was wearing a fish pin on the lapel of his jacket. On enquiring if he was a Christian he confirmed that he was. At this news my heart was somewhat gladdened as I told him that I too was a Christian and shared with him how apprehensive I was feeling about having the surgery. He assured me that he would be praying for me and that I would be given the best possible care.

With the words of my granddad's hymn still on repeat in my mind I was wheeled into surgery the next day with a deep sense of peace that Jesus was with me, that Father God had it all in hand and that all would be well. And indeed it was!

When I eventually came round in a private recovery room with all kinds of wires and tubes attached to me I became aware that my lovely husband, looking somewhat pale faced, was sitting in an armchair at my side. The nurses later joked with me how they had kept their eye on him as well as me, as he had insisted on staying by my side, whilst looking like he was going to faint at any minute!

I was in hospital for about a week and compared to some of the other ladies who had undergone the same surgery as me I considered myself blessed. Some of them were unable to stand upright for days, whilst all I could do was totter, at least I could stand tall!

It was when I got home from hospital that I began to process the events of the previous few months. Having recuperation and rest forced upon me there was little I could do but sit and ponder about things. I realised that I had done most of my grieving for my dad whilst I was nursing him and just marvelled at how God had provided for me and cared for me constantly pouring His love upon me and had led me safely through this whole difficult time. So the recuperation period became a season of thanksgiving to Father God for all His goodness towards me.

I was surrounded by the love of caring family and friends who came and visited me and brought me flowers and get well cards and helped out in whatever way they could. I had so many get well cards but there were five that had pictures of cats or kittens on them from friends who knew that at heart I am a cat lover. I put these on the hearth so I could enjoy their sweet little faces and as I looked at them I acknowledged to God how I appreciated the cards and how cute I thought they were and how I wished they were real.

Little did I know the blessing God had in store for me!

My neighbour came in each morning to make me a coffee and check on me. One morning she came in all of a fluster holding a tiny kitten in the palm of her hand and told me it had just appeared from behind my garden shed. Going into the garden to investigate we stood in amazement as a further three kittens emerged from behind the shed followed by a mother cat!

We made a bed for them out of a big cardboard box and put it under the kitchen table placing the kittens in it, the mother cat got the idea that it was for her and her babies and quickly settled in it. Although it took her a while to build up trust with humans, she was particularly distrustful of women so I think must have suffered abuse from one at some time.

Caring for the kittens and watching them grow and building up trust with the mother cat really was such a therapeutic part of my physical and emotional healing.

As I pondered over this with God and marvelled at how I hadn't even prayed and asked for kittens but had just said I *wish* the ones on the cards were real.

Every time I read John 15 verse 7 'If you remain in me and my words remain in you, ask whatever you *wish*, and it will be given you,' I am reminded of the kittens and the extraordinary things that God sometimes does to demonstrate His love to us. (I would just add that we eventually found homes for three of the kittens and kept the mother cat and one kitten. They both became part of our family and brought us a lot of happiness for many years.)

A few years later I had to undergo tricky surgery to have a lymphoma removed from my neck. Again I was apprehensive about going in for surgery when God did a most amazing thing to let me know that He was watching over me and caring for me.

In preparation for going into hospital I had a day out with a friend on a shopping trip out of town to look for a dressing gown. We trawled the shops but I couldn't see anything at all that I liked so I came home empty handed. On the way home I commented to my friend that what I would really like is a red fleecy dressing gown like the red fleecy hoody that I was wearing that day, something I could snuggle into.

The very next day I was in town doing my usual errands, when taking a short cut through a store there hanging in front of my eyes was a full length hooded red zip-up fleecy dressing gown! Exactly what I had described to my friend! I could scarcely believe my eyes! Needless to say I bought it. To this day I cannot help but think that my Father God had someone design that dressing gown with me in mind.

It was such an incredible demonstration of His awesome faithfulness and personal love towards me. When I wore it I felt that I was snuggled in His love, safe in His care and so came through surgery again His perfect love casting out all fear! (1 John 4 verse 18)

Point to ponder: Whilst none of us would choose to go through daunting times, we all do: it is a part of life in this fallen world. It is in these times when we are honest with God and pour out our fears and insecurities, hopes and desires to Him that we grow in intimacy with Him. At least that has been my experience.

Chapter 22

Wind of Change

Having fully recovered from surgery and adapted to no longer having my dad here to care for, it was time for me to seek God regarding His plans for the new season my life was entering.

As I said in an earlier chapter I had been preparing for this time by doing some theological studies with the view of going on to do further ministerial training, believing this was God's direction for me.

However as I spent time in God's presence asking Him to make His will known to me and direct my paths I increasingly felt that He was leading me to take a different direction. More and more I felt that He was calling me to do some kind of care work and less and less I felt the drawing I had once felt towards some kind of ordained ministry.

I decided that probably the only way I would find out would be to give caring work a try and trust that God would reveal His will to me as I did so. I signed up with a couple of nursing agencies and was quickly put to work and given some shifts caring for people in their own homes. As I settled in to the job I just knew in my heart that this is what I was supposed to be doing.

I had kept the Priest informed right through it all regarding the quandary I was having as to what way I was being led to go and so, eventually feeling that God was clearly showing me, I had a meeting with him and the curate to discuss it.

Having journeyed with me over some years as I had been considering ministry, he was understandably disappointed that God now seemed to be leading me in another direction. As I was speaking to him God gave me a mental picture that made it very clear to us all. I saw myself in a sailing boat sailing towards a destination that I thought I knew was exactly where I should be going.

Then the wind changed direction and I found myself being swept in another direction towards an unexpected destination. The picture was a perfect analogy of what I was experiencing, I thought I had known exactly where I was heading and then the Holy Spirit blew a wind of change that was completely altering my course. This reminds of the words of Proverbs 16 verse 9 'In his heart a man plans his course, but the Lord determines his steps.'

So instead of studying theology I found myself going to college and studying and gaining a City & Guilds qualification in Community Care. After a period of time the agencies I worked for offered me some hospital shifts and I began to work as a Health Care Assistant on the wards where there were staff shortages. This certainly broadened the spectrum of variety in my work; one day I could be doing home visits in the community which were usually low key and mainly uneventful, another day I would find myself running like a headless chicken with the demands of a busy ward with all kinds of drama going on.

Although I enjoyed the community work I found that I preferred the frenetic pace of working in the hospital and also found that in a strange way, the work was easier to switch off from! In the community I would sometimes visit clients knowing that they would be left on their own until the next carer went in at whatever time, often being left alone overnight. Of course it was the clients' choice and right to be cared for in their own homes, but many times I would be thinking of them when I was off duty, hoping they were OK, whereas when I finished a hospital shift I knew I was leaving people with ongoing care. This eventually led me to getting a full time post in the hospital and working for several years as a Health Care Assistant on an acute medical ward.

Life throughout that period of time was pretty full-on: as well as work there were lots of things going on our family life. We were blessed with two of our boys presenting us with five grandchildren within as many years. Often when I wasn't at work we would have the three little ones belonging our eldest son stay for sleepovers and on the odd occasion it would be all five of the little ones. These were special times of cousins bonding and making memories of having fun at Nanny's house. How important it is to make happy memories!

This was also a time when God began to stir up within me an interest in working with young people.

One of our close friends had become Pastor of a local church in town that was very multi-cultural in make-up. My husband was keen to support him, so we found ourselves becoming increasingly involved with the ministry in his church, especially in working with the young people. I found myself in particular working with and supporting young Asian girls. Frequently after I finished a late shift on the ward I would respond to a request to go and visit one of them. No matter what time of night it was I was always shown such warm hospitality and found myself enjoying home cooked curry or a snack of some kind while we discussed whatever was on their minds at the given time.

One outstanding memory I have is of doing a Bible study with one of the girls in the home of her married sister. As we shared our faith and discussed whatever it was that we were studying, the sister was hovering around doing small chores. Suddenly I felt the Holy Spirit interrupt my thoughts and say, 'She wants to know Jesus.' I put the study book down and looking at her I told her what I felt I had heard and asked if that was right. She immediately responded with a resounding affirmation that I had heard correctly and we had the joy of praying with her to accept Jesus as her own personal Saviour.

It is only as I look back upon this period that I am in awe at the physical and emotional energy and spiritual zeal that God gave me to serve Him in these varied capacities all at the same time! What I did not realise at the time was that He was shaping me, deepening my heart of compassion and expanding my knowledge of and love for people of other cultures.

Because our town has a large Italian community we would regularly have elderly Italian patients on the ward, who spoke little English. They would always enjoy a chat with the Italian ward cleaner, so I asked her to teach me a few Italian words. It was a joy at the end of a late shift to be able to go over to them and see their faces light up as I said 'Buona notte, Dio ti Benedica' to them [Goodnight, God Bless].

From this, a desire grew within me to go on holiday to Italy. I was in need of a holiday and as my husband was unable to get any time off work he suggested I should go to the travel agent and enquire about coach tours. Before I knew it I had a holiday booked, flights to and from Italy with a coach tour round the major cities. I was a little apprehensive of what age range my travelling companions would be, as I knew I would be prone to go into caring mode if there was need and I really was ready for a good break and time of refreshment. I committed all my apprehensive thoughts to God and trusted that He would meet my needs and He most certainly did!

On the plane going out I found myself sitting next to a young Australian girl. We hit it off right away and told the tour guide that we would be happy to share twin bedded rooms on our travels, rather than be paired up with someone who we hadn't met. That was one concern taken care of.

Two other young Australian girls on the flight introduced themselves to us and by the time we arrived in Italy we had all hooked up and become friends. It turned out to be one of the best and most relaxing holidays I have ever had! Although I was old enough to be their mother, they treated me as one of the girls and included me in all of their plans. Everything was taken care of for me from the sightseeing to where we ate. I didn't have to think about a thing. All I had to do was enjoy myself!

There were so many sights to see and joyous experiences to be had. When we were walking the quaint back streets of Venice we could hear an amazing tenor voice echoing and resounding through the streets and alleys as though serenading us. Eventually this tall stature of a man wearing a black top hat on his head and black cape draped over his shoulders came in to view, strutting with a cane in hand filling the air with magnificent song. It is a scene that will be ever etched in my mind!

Having read about the life of St. Francis, it was a dream fulfilled when we visited Assisi and the Basilica of San Francesco (St. Francis). The following year Assisi and the Basilica suffered quite a lot of damage caused by an earthquake.

There really was no mistaking God's hand of blessing upon this holiday. I was blessed beyond my wildest dreams and my appetite was whetted to dream more about further travel and adventures with God.

In the months that followed I found the bits of church youth work and pastoral care that I did in my spare time to be ever increasing. This, combined with a desire to gain some training in youth work and evangelism, led me to reduce my contracted hours at the hospital. I now had time and opportunity to do several teaching seminars with an organisation known as YWAM (Youth With A Mission). I was more like a granny with a mission! It was whilst doing a short residential Bible School with them that I met Peggy, a lady in her sixties whose testimony certainly demonstrated that age is no barrier to God. She had felt called by God in her mid fifties to join YWAM, leave her family and give up her home in America to serve God with YWAM in Amsterdam. The passion this lady had for Jesus was plain for all to see and was quite infectious.

The following year my husband and I visited her when we went with a YWAM outreach team on a short term mission trip to Amsterdam. It was an exciting time of spiritual growth through some challenging experiences, serving God in different capacities, some out of our comfort zones. This was the one and only time I have done an open air preach in the street!

One of the biggest blessings for us was that we had been able to take a young girl from our youth group with us. It was such a privilege to see how the experience, along with Peggy's testimony deepened her faith walk with God.

The dilemma that followed was that the more experiences I had of mission related things the more unsettled I became about work. I enjoyed the perks that came with earning money and being able to bless my family with treats. I began to pray about how I was feeling and recognised God's tugging and knew that once again He was gently blowing a wind of change. It seemed ludicrous in the natural to give up an income and a secure job, yet like Peggy, I knew the way God had led me thus far had proven beyond doubt that obedience to His will always brings blessing. So after much prayerful consideration I handed in my resignation to follow God's plan in whatever He had lined up for me next.

Although I confess that in doing this I hadn't completely stepped out in faith, as I had given myself a safety net by staying registered on the hospital bank. In the months that followed every time the coordinator called me to ask if I was available to do a shift on a particular day I never was available. Eventually convicted by the Holy Spirit, I confessed to the coordinator who I knew was a Christian that what I was doing wasn't honouring to either God or her and resigned from that too.

Chapter 23

New Adventures

> 1 Samuel 2 verse 30
> Those who honour Me, I will honour.

Once I had released myself from the safety net that I had been hanging on to and allowed God to lead me I found Him to be true to His word that He indeed honours those who honour Him. (1 Samuel 2 verse 30)

In the season that followed He never failed to provide for my needs and blessed me in many ways beyond anything I could ever have dreamt of. I am always amazed at how small steps of obedience can lead to tremendous blessing.

Something I saw as a small step of obedience was following God's leading to enrol at a Bible School that was being run by a local church in town. I found the topics that were covered throughout the course to be so inspiring and I enjoyed learning about the early church, the Kingdom of God, worship, interpreting scripture, preaching and so on. I gained many blessings through doing the course and made some wonderful new friends; some of whom were used by God to open doors of opportunity for me to go to new places and gain new experiences.

Whilst attending the Bible School I was challenged by God to take another step of obedience when one of the leaders of the school asked if anyone would offer hospitality to some church leaders who were coming from Kenya to attend a leadership conference in the UK. Although hospitality isn't high up in my gifting I felt God would have me respond to the request.

As a result of this we had the most amazing, humble Kenyan man of God come to stay with us, through whom I was to learn a lot.

One thing I learned was hospitality. I have always kind of thought of hospitality as being able to prepare a fatted calf at a moment's notice, which some people can seem to do! I guess I have always felt envious of people who can provide a banquet fit for a king whenever visitors turn up unexpectedly. So I had to work through in my mind that God had asked me to offer hospitality, therefore I would trust Him to bring the right person to our home who would fit in to our simple way of life. He most certainly did!

Normally speaking we would have either cereal or toast for breakfast, however for our guest I provided a selection of cereals as well as toast and various preserves. I was so taken back when he gazed at the simple spread before him and asked if this was the normal amount of food we would eat for breakfast and went on to say that it was equal to the amount that he would eat in one day at home! I was so thankful that I hadn't opted to cook a full English!

Breakfast times with him are treasured memories of joyful times of laughter and discussion, when we would discuss scriptures and share some of the joys and struggles of where we were at on our Christian journey. God certainly used this man to affirm me, encourage and motivate me and bring me to a place of deeper understanding regarding spiritual warfare, worship, intercession and the prophetic. I look back on it as a time when I felt I had sat and breakfasted with Jesus!

His visit also had quite a profound effect on our sons as they listened to stories about his cultural way of life. They were reminded of how when they were small I would encourage them to eat the food I had prepared for them, telling them how fortunate they were, that there were children in Africa who had no food at all and were starving to death. We were all impacted by the humility, love, joy and compassion of Jesus that poured forth from this man of God and one of our sons rededicated his life to Jesus as a result.

Equally our Kenyan friend was impacted by what he saw and heard about the brokenness in our British culture, broken down marriages, broken down relationships, leading to broken down families. A friend and I took him to town one Saturday evening to experience the club culture on the streets. The result was he was totally shocked and was reduced to tears by what he saw; the drunkenness and particularly the lack of modesty in the clothes worn by young girls.

By the time he left to return home it was as though God had imparted to us a love and compassion for each other's cultures and nations.

Ours being so materially rich yet so spiritually poor and theirs being so materially poor yet so spiritually rich.

The blessings from that one small step of obedience in offering hospitality multiplied in ways that I could never have imagined.

The following year my husband and I were able to go to Kenya and visit him and his family as we celebrated our silver wedding anniversary. Whilst we were there I learnt the true meaning of hospitality and what a simple life-style is in reality; the Pastor's wife washed my hair outside in the garden in a bowl of water drawn from the well and the sunshine dried it off.

The Pastor took me trekking to visit families living in mud huts in outlying villages, many of whom had suffered the loss of loved ones through the AIDS virus.

One family I visited was three young girls; the eldest aged thirteen who was left to look after the youngest about four and one in between after they had lost both parents to AIDS. It was the saddest sight to behold as they showed me the flowers they had planted on the graves of their parents in front of their mud hut. It was one of those times in life when there are no words. All I had to offer them was the overwhelming compassion and love of Jesus that was overflowing from my heart for them.

As we visited families, we invited them to come to church on the following Sunday where it had been arranged that I would preach. What we didn't know was that the church had planned a surprise for us on the Sunday. There was a young couple in the church that who were to be married that weekend and when they heard that we were celebrating twenty-five years of marriage they had a cake made especially to share with us for our special occasion. So not only did I have the joy and privilege of preaching and sharing the love of Jesus with these lovely people, but we also got to have our marriage blessed and to celebrate our silver wedding true Kenyan style by feeding each other cake, whilst our hearts overflowed with thanksgiving to God for his faithfulness to us throughout the years.

Point to ponder: Are there any small steps of obedience God may be asking you to take? Is there anything that God is asking you to let go of?

Chapter 24

I Love to Dream

Maybe because of my own testimony of how I was deceived by the enemy of my soul in my adolescent years, God grew a passion in me to see young people deepen their love walk with Jesus.

I was really blessed to be part of a youth team of likeminded people who were equally passionate about seeing young people grow in the knowledge of God's Word and His personal love for each of them. As I served God in this capacity He surprised me by opening doors that increased my vision and broadened my horizons concerning young people.

I was privileged when a friend asked me to accompany her to a wedding in Israel – Palestine. The whole experience was amazing! Staying in the local community and experiencing the culture brought scripture alive to me. Several nights of partying led up to the wedding day where the streets echoed with music, joy and gladness and then the actual wedding day when the bridegroom came to take his bride from her mother and family home and together they led the wedding procession to church for the ceremony.

For those of us who love Jesus, what a picture, we know that one day Christ will be returning to take us, His bride, home to be with Him forever!

In the midst of all the partying, God really touched my heart when a group of young girls came over to me and asked me about my love walk with Jesus. They then asked me to draw away with them from the partying to a quieter place where they wanted to show me something. What they wanted to show me was their own expression of their united love for Jesus as they worshipped Him through dance whilst singing 'My Jesus, My Saviour'. What a joy and privilege it was to witness this! In awe I asked them how they had learned to worship Jesus in such a beautiful way and was told that they had been attending a small youth project in a nearby village run by YWAM.

Another door of blessing that opened for me was when I responded to an invitation to attend a youth conference in Italy. A young guy who I knew from the local church felt called by God to start up a youth ministry in Italy. A friend and I felt God speaking to us both quite individually that we should go out to support him by attending the conference that was to be the launch of the ministry.

The conference was over a weekend and was quite a commitment as we were both working full time Monday to Friday. With this in mind we had decided to pace ourselves through the conference and miss the last session to allow ourselves plenty of time to get to the airport in a relaxed manner. However just as we were preparing to leave after lunch on the final day my friend had the strongest sense that we should stay to the last session and knowing that God had clearly led us to be there, we decided to stay to the end.

Nothing could have prepared me for how God was about to speak to me!

The worship band was made up of a group of young musicians and although I didn't understand the language their hearts of worship definitely drew us all in to the presence of God. As they began to lead us in worship a young girl who was a vocalist courageously spoke out and said although she had never done it before she felt

God had given her a word for someone in the room. She went on to say that pink was her favourite colour. It is also mine, so my ears were pinned back. She said during the week she had seen a pretty pink top in a shop window and simply could not resist buying it for herself; it was not until she had got it home and looked at it properly that she realised written on it were the words 'I love to dream'. By now I was nearly falling off my chair!

She continued that she believed God was saying there was someone who had been carrying a dream for a long time and has been wondering if it will ever come to pass and that He wanted them to know that it was soon to come to pass, or maybe it just had. She related it to the story of Jesus at the wedding of Cana of how when they had run out of wine Jesus stepped in and turned the water to wine. He had saved the best till last and that was what He was saying to whomever – He has saved the best till last!

Now why was I nearly falling off my chair! The day before we flew out to the conference I was in a store where I saw some pretty pink pyjamas and, seeing as I was going away for the weekend, I decided to treat myself to them. Written all over them were the words 'I love to dream'!

To this day I think that is one of the most powerful prophetic ways that God has ever spoken in to my life, and most definitely I walk in the fulfilment of it. God so blessed me through following Him in obedience to go to that conference and has so blessed the young guy who followed God's leading to go and plant a youth ministry that has now grown in to a powerful youth movement widely spread across Italy known as 'Youth Alive Italia'. I hope the young girl who brought that word is still dreaming and prophesying.

I think a lifelong constant dream for me has been and is, about following God. He has so many adventures for us if we will just take the time to sit in His presence and listen for His direction. We just never know where the next step will lead us. Looking back now I can see how when I have taken one step in obedience to the leading of the Holy Spirit, quite unbeknown to me God has been at work preparing me for the next step. For example whilst I was still involved in church youth work I felt drawn to secular youth work in the community, eventually I followed the leading and decide to visit a youth club that was held in the local community centre and was run by the council. This opened the door for me to get involved and work with young people in the local community in a paid capacity. After this, one remarkable step seemed to follow one after the other. The government brought out the initiative for the role of Learning Mentors to work in schools. As I was already strategically placed working in the local community, I was able to progress and be employed by a local school, where I trained and qualified as a Learning Mentor. Whilst I enjoyed this work I felt that working with a child to remove barriers to learning was limited as I wasn't engaging with the whole family. So the following year when another government initiative was launched for family workers to be placed in schools I moved into that role, working in several schools in my local area, whilst studying and gaining a qualification in Learning, Development and Support.

At the time I was just getting on with it and was somewhat surprised to find myself working in secular employment. I had always envisioned my work would be serving God somehow within a church role.

However I did have the sense that the season may have something to do with preparing me for retirement - I was thinking in monetary terms in that I was paying into a pension pot that would at least be a small boost to my state pension when the time came. It is only now as I am retired that I see the big picture and am amazed at the precision with which the Holy Spirit prepared me for this season; as I mentor, encourager and supporter of individuals and families within the church family.

Point to ponder: What are your dreams? Wherever you find yourself now - know God is preparing you for the next step on your journey with Him.

Chapter 25

God's Spirit Beckons

Romans 8 verse 14 (The Message)
God's Spirit beckons. There are things to do and places to go.

I often marvel at some of the ways that God has directed my path and pondered as to why He has chosen to speak to me through dreams and visions rather than just speaking clearly to me about what He wants me to do.

This was certainly the case when He led me to join a church that I have now been blessed to be part of for the last eight years. I was at the time feeling unsettled following the death of two Pastor friends who had taken me under their wings and had been great mentors to me, and was feeling unsure of where I was to make my spiritual home church-wise.

It began with a random dream where I just saw two capital letters BB. I felt the dream was from God but despite asking I didn't get any revelation as to the meaning of it.

Although I did sense that maybe it was something directive to do with the future. I had felt God speaking to me through His Word as I read from Romans 8 verse 14 'God's Spirit beckons' (The Message). There are things to do and places to go and Isaiah 43 verses 18-19 'Forget the former things; do not dwell on the past. See, I am doing a new thing! Now it springs up; do you not perceive it?' There was a sense in my spirit that there was something new coming but I certainly had no perception of what it was!

To add to this there were several occasions when I was worshipping in church and I would get a picture come to mind of a nearby village church with people worshipping with flags at the front of the church.

The only past connections I had with this particular church was a funeral I had attended there and once when I had gone as part of a worship group to lead worship at a churches together celebration. Not understanding what the picture was about, I kind of assumed that God must want me to pray for this particular church. However it was when I was away at a conference out of town and the same picture came to my mind as I worshipped that I began to think there was something more significant than praying for the church that God wanted me to see. I also sensed as I worshipped that Jesus was calling me to come up higher and follow Him; then someone said that as they had watched me worshipping it was as if they could see oil being poured over me.

Following the conference, I spent the next few weeks pondering over what the repeated picture was all about and finally came to the conclusion that I would pay a visit to the church on the following Sunday and see if I gained any revelation.

What I felt on that first visit was a clear sense of it being God's leading and that this is where He would have me be.

The people were friendly and welcoming, however I did question whether it really could be that God was calling me to be part of a church that was a fifteen minute drive out of town. After I had reconciled in my mind that a fifteen minute drive was not the other side of the planet, I decided that I would follow what I believed to be God's leadings and return the next

Sunday, asking that when I did that He would give me some kind of confirmation that I was hearing Him right.

When I returned the following Sunday there was a visiting preacher who is well respected for his prophetic ministry and Bible teaching especially pertaining to end times. I was aware that he had led several teaching and prophetic trips to Israel; several years prior I had had a burning desire to attend a prophetic gathering that he had led on Mount Carmel over one Easter but the door hadn't opened up for me to go. So I was feeling very blessed and privileged that by following God's leadings I now got to sit under this man's ministry for the morning, which happened to be Pentecost Sunday.

At the end of the service he said just in case anyone was interested in going that later in the year, due to his age, he would be leading his final teaching tour to Israel. Immediately my heart leapt at the thought of it and I just knew in my heart that this was God's appointed time for me to go. There was a strong sense in my Spirit that this was 'one of the things to do and places to go' that God had planned out for me.

I received the invitation as a Pentecost gift from my Heavenly Father and a clear confirmation I had been hearing Him correctly. This was the church He wanted me to be part of. (Incidentally the initials of the church are BB!).

In His grace, God gave me further confirmations too. I had a dream one night that I was on a central road that had slip roads going off to the left and the right and I was exhorting people not to veer off but to stick to the central road. A week later I was reading Deuteronomy in The Message and knew God was confirming the dream through chapter 5 verses 32-33 'So be very careful to act exactly as God commands you. Don't veer off to the right or the left. Walk straight down the road God commands so that you'll have a good life and live a long time in the land that you're about to possess.'

A couple of weeks later I was reading in the Bible how before Moses died God took him up Mount Nebo and allowed him to look out over the promised land. The way Deuteronomy 34 verse 4 is worded in The Message ripped at my heart when God said to Moses, 'I've let you see it with your own eyes. There it is. But you're not going to go in.'

At the time I was preparing to go to a youth conference in Italy and all I could think of was 'poor Moses' what a sad end to his life. This stirred me up to fervently pray that God would cleanse me and forgive me of anything that would rob me of the full inheritance that is mine in Christ Jesus!
(A good prayer to pray!)

Having done this I went off to Italy for the weekend conference. At the end of the conference the main speaker came over to me and asked if he could pray for me, as he believed God had given him a picture for me. He said he saw me like Moses standing on the top of Mount Nebo viewing the land and God was saying 'Come down, enter the promised land, it's yours!' I am still in awe as I think back on the experience. No-one but God Himself knew about the conversations I had had with Him the week before!

One day in the following weeks, as I was praying and asking God if this was connected with the move to the new church, I felt Him say to me 'I have taken you there to bless you'.

I could not deny I was experiencing God's hand of blessing and favour in so many ways. Such as, when the car I had been driving ceased up beyond repair and I needed to replace it quite urgently. Knowing that the time was coming when I would need another car, I had been saving up for this. I had asked God for a specific model, in a specific colour and had a specific amount of money saved with which to buy one; my husband being aware of my prayers looked online to see if there was anything that fitted the bill. Much to our amazement there was one that exactly met all the criteria and part of the registration plate was OMG. I declared to my husband that our car is supplied by Our Mighty God!

The next day we travelled across country to look at it and take it for a test drive. Of course there was no doubt in my mind that this was the car for us. As we chatted with the owner whilst exchanging paperwork and payment I felt God clearly say to me that I should testify and tell him and his family that we were Christians and how blessed I was by them, because the car was a specific answer to prayer. They listened in amazement and then told us that they had originally advertised the car at a higher price and had reduced it literally minutes before we had seen it advertised, explaining that they needed a quick sale because they were relocating to their family home in Delhi.

Imagine our total surprise when we got a phone call from them later that day inviting us to go and visit them in Delhi, all expenses paid apart from flights. Alas, all our savings had gone on buying the car but we were overwhelmed by their kindness and generosity and recognised it as God's hand of blessing and favour upon us.

However it was later in the year when I went on the teaching trip to Israel and Jordan that I knew without doubt that God had surely directed my paths and taken me to the place where He wanted me to put down roots and serve Him.

Although the trip was a fulfilment of a long-awaited dream to walk where Jesus walked, to sit under good Bible teaching at the same time was an added blessing. I felt strongly that the trip was very much about God's appointed time to minister into my life and prepare me for a new season of service. Three significant things come to mind when I think about the trip:

I was able to receive some prayer ministry from one of the leaders that brought me healing and freedom from a painful memory of the past that I had been carrying around. I actually literally found myself standing on top of Mount Nebo looking out across the so called Promised Land that God had shown to Moses. As I am sure you can imagine after all I had meditated on in previous months this was quite an emotional moment for me. I have to admit it looked rather more like a barren wilderness than a land flowing with milk and honey. Never-the-less it was quite a sacred moment for me.

The third thing was when we took a boat trip out on the Sea of Galilee and the leader was teaching and ministering to us from Ezekiel 47. As I stood in the boat, looking out at the water, lapping up the warmth of the sunshine and listening to the teaching I felt a powerful anointing of the Holy Spirit giving me revelation that this was a word for the church at home.

I returned to church from the trip and shared with the leadership and the church as a whole that I had an expectancy that God was at some point in time going to release the river of His presence and glory amongst us and that souls would be saved. Where the river flows there will be large numbers of fish. By this time I had no doubt whatsoever that this church was where I should be and felt quite excited about whatever God had in store for us as a church family.

Chapter 26

Putting Down Roots

Colossians 2 verses 6-7
So then, just as you received Christ Jesus as Lord, continue to live in Him, rooted and built up in Him, strengthened in the faith as you were taught and overflowing with thankfulness.

Having accepted that I was where God had called me to be, I began to settle in and explore the reasons for Him taking me there.

One thing I discovered was that at the time the church was just about to do a church plant and about the only person I knew of before going there was about to leave with her husband to lead it. She naturally asked me if I thought God was calling me to go with them but there had been no mistaking at all in that I was in fact where God had called me to be.

It is only in retrospect that I can see God's hand at work in encouraging the church that as they were releasing workers into the harvest field to go and plant a church, He was bringing other workers in, of whom I was one.

I quickly got involved in church life, going on the rota for toilet cleaning duties, helping out with young people's work and getting involved with helping to lead Alpha. Really just rolling my sleeves up and helping out wherever there was need within the capacity of my gifting and capabilities. How easy it is for us to do this.

However in all the busyness of doing, God in His grace began to speak to me about part of the reason I was there was about my being in Him. I felt Him clearly speaking to me from Psalm 1 about paying attention to the season of life that I was in. He began to show me that He was more concerned about the depths of my roots in Him than the height of my branches, the areas of service that can be seen.

I had a sense that He was saying to me that I would yield fruit for Him in due season but that this was foremost a season of me to deepen my roots in Him.

There were many experiences that God took me through that year that all served to deepen my roots in Him; some were painful and some were pleasurable.

The most painful one of all was when our great niece, Jess, the daughter of my husband's nephew, died from complications following a routine tonsillectomy, aged just four years old.

It was agonising to watch the raw grief of young parents and the family whose world had been ripped apart and changed forever by this tragedy. The day after she died I recall being in church with tears streaming down my cheeks as I felt the pain and anguish of her parents but was so helpless. As we worshipped I felt God assuring me that He too saw and felt the pain everyone was experiencing. Then as we sang 'Blessed be Your Name on the road marked with suffering when there is pain in the offering', all I could do was raise my hands in worship to Him.

It was an occasion I look back on as a milestone, as I remember how, with my hands raised in worship, I struggled to sing those words because I was crying so much. God was teaching me to worship Him in spirit and in truth regardless of whatever the situation I may find myself in.

It was soon after this that I attended an in-house leadership training day where the Holy Spirit began to highlight some things to me.

During the worship as I opened up my heart in adoration to Him, I knew it was one of those days ordained by God for Him to do business in my heart. I was challenged to examine my own life and walk with God as I listened to the teaching from the word which was based upon the life of Moses and how Moses was given a vision of God, a vision for God's people, a vision for himself and a promise from God that He would always be with him.

I had to take a truthful look at what I believed to be the call of God on my own life and what I was doing with the vision that I believed He had given me. He brought back to mind how several weeks prior I had felt Him gently speaking to me about not laying down the desires of my heart regarding

Kenya and for sharing the Word but I hadn't paid much attention to it at the time.

Now gently but surely God was revealing to me how I had allowed pain and disappointment from some things that I had experienced to dampen what I believed to be God's call on my life. During the ministry time that followed I shared what God had been revealing to me and felt cleansed of all hurt and disappointment as I wholeheartedly repented and was prayed for, prophesied over and anointed with oil.

Following the training day I felt that God was leading me to cut down the hours of paid work that I was doing. I sensed as I read a few words of David's prayer for his son Solomon asking that God would give his son an uncluttered and focussed heart so that he could obey what the Lord commanded and live by His direction and counsel. (See 1 Chronicles 29) Maybe God wanted to remove some clutter from my life work-wise.

At the time I was working part time hours supporting families across three schools. After giving it some prayerful consideration, I decided to drop one of the schools.

As is often the way, after I had given in my notice the enemy tried to put doubt in my mind as to if I had really heard God. On my last day in the school I had an amazing affirmation from God through some Bible reading notes for that particular day: 'Go overboard for the Lord. Whatever you give up He will repay many times over. Whatever you are willing to walk away from ultimately determines what He can trust you with.'

How good and awesome is God!

Sometime later in the year I found myself in Italy once again, having felt to go and show support to my friend who was running another youth conference.

Or at least I thought that the reason I was there! However soon after I arrived and had settled in my hotel room, as I sat giving God thanks for His abundant goodness and for giving me the opportunity to be there I felt Him say that He had brought me away to come aside with Him; it was a time to rest and enjoy His company.

Although there was glorious sunshine outside and a conference running, most of my time was spent in my room in solitude enjoying companionship with my Father and Jesus, the lover of my soul. As we spent time together the Holy Spirit powerfully ministered to my heart about my identity in Him and affirming my uniqueness created by Him for His glory. Below is part of how I summarised the trip in my prayer journal:

- I value my uniqueness and I know you do too
- I value my need for solitude – time alone with you

- I value the anointing you have given me to be extravagant in expressing my worship to you in private and in public
- I value the boldness you have given me to speak out for you and the courage you have given me to follow you where-ever and enjoy your company where-ever
- I value my life and all you have filled it with – my marriage, my children, my grandchildren and every single blessing you have blessed me with.

I am still filled with awe when I think about that trip and consider the lengths God will go to in pouring out His love upon us; enabling us to grow in intimacy with Him. The trip was definitely one pleasurable experience of deepening my roots in Him, one that I will never forget.

Point to ponder: Consider writing down the things that make you unique and reflect on them and celebrate who you are.

Chapter 27

Gold Dust

In the months following what can only be described as my Italian retreat, I felt God speaking to me as I reflected upon the life of Abraham. How he didn't know the plan God had for his life, he didn't know where he was heading but he just walked in obedience as God directed him. I felt I related to Abraham in that I had followed God by starting out on a journey of obedience not understanding at all His direction, but following any way, really walking in blind faith.

I wrote in my prayer journal: 'I am here because you Lord have led me here. I know that you will fulfil your plan and purpose for me being here.' Actually it is like watching an exciting movie – I want to know what happens next. I feel as though I am on a voyage of discovery.

One day during a time of worship I had a picture of the church where I attend but it looked more like an attractive upmarket hotel, all along the front of it there were flagpoles with flags flying from them. I felt God say that it was about 'expansion' and that as people are drawn to a smart hotel people will be drawn to the church.

I pondered on the picture and wondered if there was a connection with the Ezekiel 47 scripture that God had given me for the church when I was in Israel.

I was at a conference shortly after this when I felt God underlining to me the importance of everyone being in the right place of service according to the gifts He had given them and I could see how that fitted with a vision of expansion.

I was really encouraged when someone asked if they could pray for my ministry and said that they felt that God had been leading me to take small steps and that nothing that happened was by chance but was planned by Him.

It was a short time after this early in 2010 when I had a very vivid dream in which someone was remonstrating me and said, 'This is the year for you to get on and follow the call that God has put on your life!' I had no doubt that God was speaking to me through the dream and was expectant for Him to give me further insight as to the meaning of it.

A few days after that, I went to the church of a friend to hear the testimony of a missionary who was serving God in Burundi. As I listened to his story of how he had felt God clearly call him to

Burundi, something resonated in my spirit and I thought to myself as surely as God had called that man to Burundi, He had called me to where He wanted me to serve Him.

I came away with affirmation that I was in the right place, being where I was in the village church and doing what I was doing by way of serving the Lord; yet I had a sense following the dream that the year ahead was going to be somehow significant.

In the following weeks I found myself reflecting upon the words of the Lord's Prayer, particularly the bit about praying for His Kingdom to come and His will to be done on Earth as it is in Heaven. As I meditated on it I felt the Holy Spirit doing a work in my heart and changing my perspective.

Being by nature a reflective person I am quite happy to spend hours alone chewing things over with God, enjoying time in His presence. The Holy Spirit brought to my mind how often I accused myself of 'being so Heavenly minded that I am no Earthly good.' He brought me gentle correction and a conviction that I needed to repent of how I had been chastising myself.

As I repented I felt Him give me revelation that to be Heavenly minded is actually the key to being a lot of earthly good. He pointed out to me that when I ask Him to use me as a channel of His blessing I am asking for His Kingdom to come and for Heaven's blessings to be released on earth.

Soon after this bit of revelation teaching; I heard someone speaking on a Christian broadcast about former great outpourings of the Holy Spirit. They were saying that they believed that God had shown them how plates in the centre of the earth were moving, causing tsunamis, earthquakes and the like; that there was a move going on in the heavens too and that this would cause Holy Spirit outpourings and manifestations on earth.

When I heard I felt my spirit as I felt it was related to what I had been meditating over in the Lord's Prayer.

I held it all before God for a few days as I pondered over what I had heard. I then decided to set aside some designated time asking that God would speak to me and give me understanding, crying out to Him that He would not allow me to be deceived.

During the time set aside I didn't hear anything or receive any revelations at all; however later in the day I was sitting in my study writing a list preparing to go shopping when a very strange thing happened. I noticed all my fingernails were glistening with a light dusting of gold and it appeared to be heaviest on my thumbnails. I began to look around to see what I had been touching, realising I hadn't been touching anything, I tried wiping it off but it just stayed there. Then came the realisation that whatever it was, it was God grabbing my attention! I sat for a while in total shock and awe.

Recalling how I had heard reports about people experiencing gold dust appear on their bodies and how sceptical I had been at some of the reports. I quickly repented of my scepticism!

After about half an hour or so, it gradually faded away and in a complete daze I got up and caught a bus into town to do my shopping. I recall sitting on the bus rubbing my fingernails and staring at them all the way to town, wondering if I had dreamt the experience. Goodness knows what anyone thought if they were watching me!

I was still in a daze when later that evening I attended my Discipleship Group which happened to be a night of sharing with each other. I sat very quiet all night asking God if I was supposed to share with the group what I had experienced earlier in the day. At the end of the evening the group leader commented that I had been unusually quiet and asked if there was something I had to share and I felt it was a prompt from God to tell them what had happened. It was quite a funny sight as they then all went quiet and looked as dazed as me.

Driving home from the meeting I was going over it all again with God and said to Him, 'If this really was you giving me a sign and speaking to me please do it again and let someone else see it'. I felt bad doubting God but was struggling to believe or understand what it was all about.

When I reached home I walked in to the kitchen and with it all swirling through my mind put the kettle on to make myself a cup of tea. If a cup of tea was supposed to help me think straight it certainly didn't this time, for as I looked down at my hands both my palms were glistening gold. I called my husband to come and look, already having told him about the experience I had had earlier in the day. He affirmed to me that I was not imaging things that my palms were indeed glistening with what appeared to be sparkles of gold dust.

I was once again in total awe and amazement. I knew God had answered the request I had made to Him as I was driving home. However I was even more amazed when I went upstairs and getting ready for bed I looked in the mirror as I was about to take off my make up and saw that there was gold glistening all around my lips. Then looking across at my Bible that was lying on my bed I noticed it too was glistening with gold dust.

Just as before, the gold gradually faded away but I was left with a tingling sensation on my lips, both palms of my hands and on the soles of my feet. That night I went to sleep singing in the Spirit and clutching my Bible that is the very Word of God which is for sure like gold to me. The whole experience left me in a state of total awe, fear and trembling that remains with me today when I think back on it.

During the weeks following, several other people experienced gold dust appearing on their hands too and at a Discipleship Group being led by the Minister, gold dust appeared on the pages of his open Bible which was then passed round the room for all to see.

What was it all about? I believe it was a season when God was manifesting His presence to us in such a way that deepened our reverence and awe of who He is! God will not be put in a box!

Chapter 28

Release of Joy

Psalm 16 verse 11
You have made known to me the path of life. You will fill me with joy in Your presence, with eternal pleasures at Your right hand.

Following the gold dust experience I began to read up on and take an interest in, people past and present who were used by God to operate in signs and wonders. I was particularly impacted by reading the story of Maria Woodworth - Etter who was mightily used by God in the realm of signs and wonders at the turn of the twentieth century. Reading about her walk with God stirred up a hunger in my own heart for getting to know Him deeper and in more intimate ways for myself. I had a definite sense of God at work in me desiring to give me greater revelation and take me up to a new level in my walk with Him.

When I heard that a church that is known for operating in signs and wonders was holding a conference locally, I decided to go along to it.

It was certainly a different experience from any other conference that I had been to. As I write now I am trying to define what made it different. I think it was the prophetic edge that came with the teaching and the corporate sense of expectancy that was in the room.

I had gone along with some friends and enjoyed spending time together with them in an atmosphere of worship in God's presence. I witnessed several people receiving prophetic words of encouragement and being blessed by the teaching, although personally I didn't feel God had revealed anything new to me.

That was, until the end of the conference when they did a fire tunnel or prayer tunnel as they are sometimes known. For the sake of anyone who is unfamiliar with what one is; it is a tunnel made up of two lines of people facing each other and joining hands in the air with the person opposite them, thus creating a tunnel. They then pray and sometimes prophesy over people as they walk through it.

I went to follow my friends through the tunnel and as I began to enter it the Pastor of the church who was putting on the conference put his hand on my shoulder and said 'In the presence of God is fullness of joy!' At which point I keeled over backwards under the power of the Holy Spirit and found myself laughing as I felt what I could only describe as being bathed in God's love.

After a short while I picked myself up and tried again to go through the fire tunnel, stopping at the entrance to try and explain to the Pastor what had just happened to me. I told him my name was Joy and there seemed to be a connection with my name and what he had spoken over me. This comes from Psalm 16 verse 11 'You will show me the path of life; in Your presence is the fullness of joy; at Your right hand are pleasures forevermore.' At which point he prayed something like 'More Lord!' and I keeled over backwards again and this time I was laughing more than ever. I was very thankful to be wearing trousers as I was kicking my legs in the air feeling totally overwhelmed by an indescribable joy. I had no sense of embarrassment just sheer joy.

It was a couple of weeks later when I sat in my Pastor's office, telling him about the experience I had had at the conference that God gave me revelation to the meaning of it all as we spoke. I described to my Pastor that when I was lying on the floor kicking my legs in the air it felt like I was a baby lying in a pram on a warm sunny day, feeling happy and contented, kicking my feet in the air and celebrating life. In that moment I knew God had done a healing work of releasing me into the fullness of all He had created me to be; of restoring to me a deep level of joy that was my birthright that through the years the enemy of my soul had sought to steal.

I then discussed with my Pastor about the possibility of later doing a year-long training course in supernatural ministry (TSM) with the church who had put on the conference. After giving it some prayerful consideration we both felt it was something that God was directing me to do and an added blessing was a friend who had come to the conference with me felt called to do it too.

Through the summer months I sought to prepare myself for the course that was due to start in the autumn. As I looked at how to plan my time management, I felt that for me to gain the most from the course that maybe it was time for me to relinquish work in another school. This didn't make sense financially as there was a cost involved in doing the course; but by the end of the summer I felt sure this was what God would have me do.

It wasn't a decision I made lightly or easily and there was business I had to do with God in the Secret Place. One concern I had was regarding the impact my leaving might have on a particular child who I had been working with for some time. I had to work through and come to the place of recognising the bottom line that I was replaceable and either I trusted God with the child's welfare or I didn't. Then there was the old taunt of 'Has God really said?' In my journal I wrote 'I feel God is pulling me forwards but I'm hanging on, fearful of letting go in case I have got it wrong!' As I read what I had written I had such a powerful revelation of how fear had the potential to stop me moving forward in to my God-given destiny. With that, I renounced fear and negative thoughts in Jesus' Name and wrote a letter of resignation to the Head Teacher.

When I went into school at the start of term to work out my notice I had a meeting with the Head and explained the reason I was leaving. I was so blessed by the encouragement she gave me about doing the course and the news she told me regarding the child I had been concerned about; they had moved area during the summer months and was therefore no longer attending the school.

On my last day at the school they put on a special school assembly for me, the children sang a song about God's love and I was presented with a beautiful bouquet of flowers and card; I came away knowing God's love was carrying me through yet another transition.

Once again I was discovering how obedience brings blessing. Going to the initial conference was like a stepping stone for me to do the course that in turn would bring me to new levels in my faith walk with Jesus.

Part of the course requirements were that we needed to have someone mentor us throughout the course with whom we could meet up regularly to discuss and reflect on how it was going; my Pastor, bless him, offered to be my mentor and journey with me. I was so grateful as he was such an encourager.

So the journey began!

One of the first things I recognised on the course was how the reading material, much about revivalists past and present was exactly what I had been craving to read.

I quickly discovered too that all the worship, teaching and making new friends with likeminded people all served to make me more passionate about guarding and deepening the intimacy I enjoy in my love walk with Jesus.
I had a real sense that God was scratching where I itched!

Chapter 29

Polishing the Arrowhead

Whilst doing the TSM course I very much felt that it was a time of preparation for whatever God had lined up for me in the future. In many ways it was a time of affirmation of things I had felt God speak in to my life over the years of walking with Him, as well as a time of cleansing, refining and growing in faith. The title for this chapter came from a prophetic word spoken over me that I was like an arrowhead being polished up ready for God to use; this just about described how I felt.

Soon after starting the course someone spoke prophetically to me and said they believed that through TSM God would reinforce words He had spoken to me about through the years. Indeed I found this to be so. I would say part of the polishing for me was learning to pay more attention to what God says whether it is through His written Word, through the still small voice, through prophesy, or dreams and visions.

Although I had kept prayer journals over the years I would rarely look at them and read some of the treasures I had written in them. In one of the teaching sessions we heard a guy share how he had written down prophetic words and scriptures that he had received over a number of years on to postcards and where-ever he went he carried them with him. He said it was a great encouragement to him to look at them and be reminded of some of the things God had spoken over his life. This was a real light bulb moment of revelation and learning for me, and something I have applied and now do myself in a similar way.

I went through my journals and wrote down on small pieces of card, key scriptures and prophetic words that were like treasures to me then put them in a small organza drawstring bag and created what I call my treasure bag.

Something I have learnt through doing it, is that it keeps alive the seeds of faith that God has planted in our hearts through the years and things that may have lain dormant for years begin to grow as we revisit them and pray over them. It is a practice that the Holy Spirit is at present nudging me to do more of.

I recall an analogy the Holy Spirit once gave me regarding seeds of faith through a conversation I had with our eldest son. He had given me a packet of tomato seeds, several weeks later he asked me how my seeds were doing. My reply was that they were still in the packet! I was immediately challenged that I needed to be more diligent with seeds of faith that I had been given!

Another practice I developed from the teaching on the TSM course was to keep a dream diary. I have found it encouraging to see how often God speaks to me through dreams and, as with the treasure cards, by writing them down I can prayerfully revisit them.

I had a very vivid dream three months into doing the TSM course about the Head Teacher of the one remaining school where I was still working part-time. I dreamt that I was on a night out with her and the school staff when I lost my purse. She was helping me to look for it and became distraught for me when we couldn't find it. I was quite calm and peaceful about the situation and told her not to worry - it was only money.

I had a strong suspicion that the dream was about God preparing me for a time when I was no longer working but I parked it for now and concentrated on what I was doing at the present time.

About six weeks after the dream the Head Teacher asked me a direct question, 'If she could obtain the funding for the following financial year would I stay?' My immediate response was that yes I would. At once my mind was thrown into turmoil and it seemed although I had parked the dream, God hadn't. I revisited it and prayed over it on my own and with the church leadership. We all agreed that the dream seemed to affirm the sense that at some point in time God was maybe going to move me on to something that He was preparing me for. I love how God uses times like this to draw us into deeper intimacy with Him. As I worshipped Him, pouring out my love for Him, resting in the knowledge that He knows my heart and He knows the plans that He has for me; I told Him my only desire was to serve Him in whatever way He sees fit and bring Him glory. I sensed the still small voice speaking to my heart, 'Stay with it.'

The thing I felt I was to stay with was just simply continuing to walk in obedience to Him and I felt Him say that as I did so, there were to be no formulas, no performance, just obedience.

I increasingly desired to spend more and more time with Him in the Secret Place. I would frequently wake in the night and be aware of the Holy Spirit ministering to me and speaking to me about things I needed to repent of, or giving me revelation teaching from the life of Jesus. All I wanted to do was hang out with Jesus whenever and where-ever I could. I recall one night when I was alone in church having been over to clean the toilets and just spent time alone prostrate before the cross, repenting and pouring out my love for Jesus asking Him to bless the church.

By the time I graduated from the TSM course I had no idea of what God's future plans for me were work wise: all I knew was that my passion was stirred up to follow Him all the days of my life, to serve Him and live for His glory and impart that passion to others!

Chapter 30

A Time of Moving On

After finishing the TSM course; with the start of a new term, I settled back in to the routine of school work and church work of helping lead Alpha groups, nurture groups and helping out with the planning of special services.

It was then I had a dream that I am sure was a warning that things were about to change.

I dreamt that I had walked into a church meeting and everyone was sound asleep, each person with their head resting on the person next to them; some were even snoring!

I had a sense that God was about to wake us up from our slumber. Indeed it proved to be so, when two weeks later the Pastor announced to the whole church family that after a time of prayerful consideration that he and his wife felt God clearly speaking to them that it was time for them to leave us and move on. This news certainly woke the church up!

Like everyone else I had to work through processing the news especially as I had worked closely with him when he had mentored me through the TSM year and encouraged me in my walk with God.

I came through to a place of acknowledging that a season had come to an end for him and for the church and was thankful to God for all I had learnt under his ministry. I was also thankful that through the years God had taught me to keep my eyes fixed upon Jesus and not upon earthly leaders. (It always concerns me when I hear people talking about following a person: I was at a conference once when someone was raving about the speaker, and telling me how they followed them, then asked me as to whom I follow? For me there was, and is, only one answer to that question and it is Jesus!) Therein was my security, I knew that I had followed Jesus and was where I was supposed to be. The important factor to me was about my obedience to God, not to who was leading the church.

I believe an encounter that I had with the Holy Spirit soon after going to the church helped to sustain me and keep me Kingdom focussed through this period of church life.

It was a Sunday morning service and I was sitting on the floor praying with the Pastor and his wife when I felt quite overcome by the power of the Holy Spirit and just had to lie down and soak in His presence. I stayed in this state for a good two hours until everyone had gone home apart from a sister who stayed behind to support me and pray with me. During the time that I was resting in the presence of the Holy Spirit I had a picture of a very vivid bright turquoise coloured river in which I was playing, inviting other women who were nearby to come and join me. From that encounter an expectation has stayed with me that the river of God would flow through the church.

It was at a church weekend when a visiting speaker said, 'Fluidity is not about having plans and strategies but about going with the flow,' that I sensed that this was some of what the vision of the river had been about. I had peace of mind about not getting caught up with plans and strategies but going with the fluidity of the river, the Holy Spirit's leadings.

Although I wasn't at all sure what the Holy Spirit's leadings were, after another vivid dream I had where I was standing at the back of the church during a presentation service, watching as the Pastor was being presented with gifts; then it was announced that I was to be presented with something too. I was being awarded a microphone and people standing around me were asked to pray for me. As I prayed about the dream I felt God saying to me that He had given me a voice to speak out.

The dream was still in my mind a couple of days later when I popped into the church office for something and there on the desk lay a golden microphone! I stared in amazement enquiring to whom it belonged. It turned out to belong to a Pastor from another church, who happened to be a parent of a child at the school where I worked; so I volunteered to take it and return it to him but not before getting someone to take a photograph as I posed with it as a tangible reminder of the dream.

The school was A Catholic school, where I returned the microphone to its owner and also sought counsel and prayer regarding the dreams I was having from a friend who was the school chaplain. She said she felt as we talked and prayed that she felt God was preparing me for a time of change that was coming and that it was time to use the gifts that God had given me, particularly the gift of words. This brought to mind the several promptings of the Holy Spirit I had had regarding writing a book and also brought back to mind the dream I had had almost a year earlier about losing my purse and not being concerned about the loss of money.

It was a very strange time for me whilst most of the church was coming to terms with the Pastor leaving I was seeking to understand what God was saying to me on a personal level. I recall one day when I was feeling particularly unsettled and wanting God to speak to me and give me some direction or understanding when a friend called me up and I shared with her how unsettled I was feeling. Immediately she said, 'I believe you are spiritually pregnant and in a nesting season.' This so resonated in my spirit as being true and the thought went through my mind as to where nine months would take me to and realised it would be exactly the end of the next school year.

I took it as a very clear sign that the time was nearing for me to retire from paid work completely; especially as I felt God confirm it to me from some daily reading notes that said, 'You must be willing to leave the safety of where you are and go where God wants to take you.'

The period I was in did very much seem to be like a nesting season of preparation. I reflected upon parallel feelings of when I had been physically pregnant with my children and how I would clean out cupboards and drawers in preparation for their birth and now it was like God wanted to clean out things in my life in preparation for whatever He was going to bring to birth spiritually in my life. One thing I felt to relinquish was the admin work that I was doing for Alpha. I had done it as there had been a need and I could do it, but it was like an ill-fitting pair of shoes that just wasn't comfortable. God began to speak to me through this about working to my strengths and encouraging others to do the same and I felt Him give me what I would describe as a kind of mandate for the future to mentor, motivate and mobilise people.

Point to ponder: Are you running the race of life flowing in your God given strengths? Maybe discuss this with a friend.

Chapter 31

What Next?

The New Year started off in a very encouraging way as my husband and I prepared and shared dreams for my retirement later in the year. I had a desire to go to visit my sister in Australia who I hadn't seen for sixteen years or so. Realising how expensive it would be to finance such a trip, in chatting to God, my Heavenly Father I asked if He would just drop £4,000 in to our bank account. Just after this I noticed on my husband's desk a letter regarding an insurance policy that had been buried under other correspondence for a while. On looking at it we realised it was something that was no longer needed and would have a cash value to it. I am sure by now you will have guessed it was £4,000 that was duly paid into our bank account, much to our joy and delight.

I had an expectancy that the year ahead was going to be an exciting one and because of the specific answer to prayer I had a quiet assurance that whatever it held that God had gone before me.

Many things were going through my mind as I pondered with God about this spiritual pregnancy, wondering what would be birthed when I finished work. One of my granddaughters had done me a prophetic painting of an open gate and me walking through it following a shadow and that is exactly how I felt. It was as though I was walking through the gate following the direction of the Holy Spirit and yet not knowing where He would lead me.

I felt that God was whetting my appetite and fulfilling some of the microphone dream by opening a few doors for me to speak at some evening services and do a brief preach in a morning service at church.

However it is one particular Saturday morning that stands out in my mind when as I was spending time in the Secret Place reading from Acts 6 about how the Apostles delegated work so that they could give their attention to prayer and ministry of the Word. As I read it I felt the Holy Spirit say, 'It's time to preach.' As I sat and pondered over what I believed I had heard, something else came to my mind that had been said to me and spoken over me several times in the couple of years prior, about me having an apostolic ministry. This I did not understand at all.

One time when I was leading a nurture group, we were talking about spiritual gifts in the church when someone new in the faith said to me that he saw me as an apostle. When I asked why on earth he said that, he replied, 'Because an apostle is someone who builds up people and people build churches.' Also someone had said to me at the time of the gold dust experience that thumbs were symbolic of apostleship. I was pondering over these things in my mind wondering if maybe somehow it was connected with the mentoring, motivating and mobilising, when I had a phone call from a sister in Christ saying that God had laid me on her heart that morning and asked if she could come round and pray for me. I invited her to come round later in the day, encouraged that God had laid me on her heart as we hardly knew one another at all. We worshipped in different churches and our only connection was a Christian ministry we were both involved in. I was in a state of absolute awe when she came round later and told me that as she had prayed for me that morning she felt that God was instructing her to come and pray a release over me to receive a prophetic apostolic anointing. Which she did! I was left pondering more than ever; one thing I could not doubt was that God speaking to me.

Soon after this one morning, quite unexpectedly, I felt God give me revelation on the spiritual pregnancy and show me it was leading prayer ministry. My immediate reaction was disbelief, I said to Him 'But I am not an intercessor,' to which I felt Him reply with a question, 'What do you do all day?'

'Oh yes – chat to you Lord!' I struggled to believe I could be hearing right as there was already someone who fulfilled that role in church, but when I questioned God on it I felt Him clearly tell me that they would be stepping down from the position. Immediately I began to pray God's blessing over that person wondering what was going on in their lives. I shared what I believed I had heard with just a couple of sisters who walked closely with me on my spiritual journey and whom I could trust to say nothing but would pray for me. Apart from that I was like Mary and pondered things over in my heart.

During the following weeks God released a barrage of affirmations, speaking to me such that it was impossible for me to ignore Him. So much so that I recorded a timeline and dated all the scriptures and affirmations so that I could meditate over all He was saying to me. Such random things happened, for example someone relatively new in the faith who I was preparing for baptism was at our home one night and we were having a wonderful prayer time together when she told me that I was the first person to ever hear her pray out loud. I was so surprised as she prayed with so much confidence and authority. On another occasion I had a phone call asking if I would go over to help a Minister to organise a prayer tent and praying in the streets of a new housing development. As it happened I wasn't free to go but I knew it was one of God's pointers for me; as was the influx of random people that turned up at my door asking for prayer.

The other thing that was going on with me was my heart was increasingly over-flowing with worship and one day as I was walking down the street to visit my granddaughter I found myself singing out in the Spirit and then sang out the interpretation:

It's a new day – it's a new day
It's a new way – it's a new way
I hold before you an open door
Stay close to me – stay close to me.

It was coming close to the end of term and true to what I believed I had heard from God, the person leading the prayer ministry stepped down from the position.

I was now feeling the weight of what I was carrying and after much seeking God, I decided that it was time for me to go and share everything with one of the Church Elders. Having left with him all I had been carrying for what was now nine months; I came away feeling lighter as though I had experienced a painless birth.

The initial period following my retirement was to say the least a little confusing for me, as the role of leading prayer ministry was given to someone else. I felt so confused as I was sure I had heard God correctly. The enemy of my soul, the great deceiver, wasted no time in trying to convince me that I had been totally deceived. I was having none of his ploys - I know the voice of my Shepherd and I had been obedient thus far in following Him and if things weren't working out for me the way I thought they would, it certainly wasn't because He was deceiving me, it was for my utmost good.

The following is an extract from my prayer diary at the time as I combated the enemy:

> Holy Spirit I am so before You – did I really hear You regarding prayer ministry? Was it my mind? Please do not allow me to be deceived, keep me in the centre of Father's will and plan for my life. Father, search my heart and cleanse me of any selfish ambition and please protect me from bitter envy. Let my life demonstrate humility that comes from Heavenly wisdom.

With my heart right before God, although still not understanding, I was able to move on in my walk with Him and trust Him with whatever plans He had for my life.

As part of my retirement celebrations I had arranged earlier in the year to visit with one of our granddaughters, a friend and sister in Christ from our church who had gone out to Kenya and had set up a home for orphaned children. In retrospect I realised how perfectly God had timed this trip. It was so special to share an exciting adventure with my granddaughter that we had planned out together over the previous months. We made new friends, I did some speaking at a ladies' meeting. We went on safari and experienced magnificent sunsets whilst watching wild animals in their natural habitat. As well as spending time with my friend and seeing first-hand how God was using her and blessing her ministry.

Then it was only a couple of months later when my husband and I went on our holiday of a life time travelling business class to Australia and New Zealand to celebrate my sixty fifth birthday. God really blessed us with such a special time visiting family and friends. The time I got to spend with my sister after not seeing each other for so many years, I will always see as one of God's precious gifts to us both. Another was when my nephew's wife took me on my birthday to a *Hillsong Sisterhood* meeting, where I not only enjoyed worshipping God with hundreds of likeminded sisters in Christ but also got the surprise of my life when I was presented with a birthday present from Bobbie Houston.

I certainly felt the start of my retirement had been hallmarked with blessing!

Chapter 32

Dreams of Revival

Psalm 57 verse 5
Be exalted, O God, above the heavens, let Your glory be over all the Earth.

As I entered a new year I also entered a new season of intimacy with Jesus. I felt the Holy Spirit constantly drawing me aside to spend time in the Secret Place to be alone with Him and feel His heartbeat as I allowed Him to pour out His love upon me.

The wonder of knowing intimate times with Jesus in the Secret Place is that it can happen anywhere, at any time, even with people all around us.

I recall a Sunday morning communion service at church at this time, when I became so lost in worship and adoration of Jesus as I knelt before Him. I felt the love pouring from my heart towards Him was how Mary must have felt when she anointed the feet of Jesus with oil. As we sang 'I receive your love' it was as though an impartation of love was being poured out over me, direct from Heaven. I felt as if my lips were being touched by Heaven's kiss.

Of course isn't this why we take communion? To remember the ultimate sacrifice that Jesus made for us when He died on the cross, paying the price for our sins so that we could know forgiveness and have assurance of eternal life. To be reminded of that great exchange of love; that the love we have for Him is only because He first loved us.

One morning at 5am when I was up praying and spending time in the Secret Place I was aware of a faint perfume filling the room and then when I opened my Bible to read my daily reading it was from Exodus 30 about the fragrant anointing oil. God had been speaking to me so much about the Bride of Christ being prepared for the return of her Bridegroom I knew the perfume was a confirmation of what I had been hearing about His desire for consecration and holiness.

I really sensed a work of God's grace going on in my life at this time as the church was in a time of interregnum. Whilst along with the whole church I was seeking God's will concerning us getting a new Pastor, I felt the Holy Spirit drawing me to keep my gaze focussed upon Jesus and rest in the knowledge that He is our true Shepherd. I also felt that the Holy Spirit was revealing to me His desire to draw all His people in to a place of deeper intimacy with Himself and I began to share it with whoever would listen. At the time, I was speaking quite regularly on Sunday evenings when intimacy with God became the underlining theme for all of my talks. My burning desire was and I must say still is, to mentor, motivate and mobilise folk in becoming more passionate to go all out for Jesus.

I was so hungry to hear from God and understand all that He was saying to me that when I saw a prophetic healing conference advertised somewhere it went through my mind as to whether it was something I should go to. Taking cost and distance into consideration with no particular direction from God about it I dropped the idea.

Then the most amazing thing happened! I was in town one day some weeks later when I bumped into a friend who I hadn't seen for a while so we decided to go and have a coffee together. As we sipped on our coffee she casually asked me if I would like to go to a conference with her saying she had a spare ticket, room booked and transport provided. I sat in utter amazement – it was the very conference that I had thought about going to! I eagerly accepted her kind offer and took it as a clear sign that for some reason I was meant to go to this conference.

I wondered if I might get revelation on several things I had been praying about and was especially curious about what God might be saying following a dream I had one night. I dreamt that I was walking back to my home from town and every church I passed was heaving with life as people were praising and worshipping God, revival had broken out right across town.

I went to the conference with the dream very much at the forefront of my mind wondering if God really was speaking to me through the dream about revival. That He was going to bring revival.

However it wasn't the conference itself, but rather the hotel where we were staying where I felt God give me affirming revelation. As I stood in the welcome lounge area, my eyes were drawn to the décor; the ceiling was decorated with artwork of gold painted fish all the way around the room. Immediately God brought to my mind the scripture from Ezekiel 47 and the word I had felt Him give me for our church when I was in Israel a few years prior. Where the river flows there will be life – this fitted with the dream and all the churches being full of life.

I returned from the conference with a sense that God was definitely giving me signs that He was speaking. This being confirmed when on my return I was telling the Youth Worker about my trip and showed him the photograph I had taken of the golden fish. He immediately recognised it to be the very room where a few years before, he along with some friends had first met to do a church plant in that town.

Another thing that I had felt God speaking to me about earlier in the year on a personal level was that He was calling me to come up higher. He gave me an analogy of learning to dive (not that I do); how you start by just jumping from the side of a pool, progressing to diving boards of increasing height, eventually diving from heights that you would never have dreamt of.

As I followed Him through the coming months I could indeed see areas where He was calling me to be brave and step up and step out in adventures with Him. I did some small group workshops on finding our identity in Christ that turned out to be rewarding times of fun with friends. I also took on leading a weekly Discipleship Group and a definite stepping up and stepping out was a return visit to Kenya where God opened doors for me to minister in a couple of churches.

One of them turned out to be stepping up experiences for sure; I was expected to preach for between one to two hours and I was the second preacher! They had two sermons and the service went on for over six hours! God was faithful and preserved me in the heat and ministered through me to the hearts of spiritually hungry people.

There was a brave moment too when I discovered a rat in my room in the middle of the night. I can never describe the Christian life to be boring!
Also while I was there I was impacted by something I saw on a church wall; it was a picture of a tree and underneath was written 'grow deep and spread far'. I realised that was exactly what had been happening to me throughout the year. He had been taking me deeper in to Him and now here I was once again sharing His love with people in Kenya. How good and awesome is our God!

Soon after I returned home I once again felt the Holy Spirit speaking to me about revival. It came as I listened to the news about a tidal power-surge that was expected to hit the country. Exceptionally high tides were expected and there were concerns and lots of speculation as to whether the sea defences would hold back the floodwaters. As I listened I felt the Holy Spirit challenging me; Was I, was His church, expecting a surge of His power to sweep over the land in answer to our prayers or had we built up strong defences in protecting ourselves from it?

This led me to pray and ask God to remove all defences in me and in His church that would hinder us being flooded with a surge of His powerful presence where souls, many souls would be saved, bodies healed and captives set free.

Throughout the year a verse that had sat with me was Habakkuk 2 verse 3 (NKJV) 'For the vision is yet for an appointed time; But at the end it will speak, and it will not lie. Thou it tarries, wait for it; Because it will surely come, It will not tarry.'

I had no clear vision at all, just a strong sense that God was speaking and that He was at work moving things into place. I remember going to a meeting at church one night and telling God how concerned I was as I didn't seem to have any particular personal vision and knowing that the Word speaks about how people without vision perish, I didn't feel like I was in a good place. That was until in our worship time we sang 'Jesus be the centre... be my vision...be my guide...be the reason that I live.' What a revelation!! Of course I had vision, Jesus alone is my central vision, He is the reason I live He is my guide and all He calls me to do is follow Him day by day I didn't need to see down the road.

Chapter 33

A New Day Dawning

Psalm 57 verse 2
I cry out to God Most High, to God, who fulfils His purpose for me.

As time went on it certainly proved to be the case that God was at work behind the scenes, moving things into place to bring us a new Pastor. Some friends of the Youth Worker who he had worked with previously in a church plant had been leading a church in the USA and had felt that God was now calling them back to serve Him in the UK. The question was raised were we the church where God was calling them to serve? After much prayer from all parties and after meeting them it was clear to all that this indeed was the case. So we found ourselves with a new Pastor. What amazed and amused me, was that he was part of the team leading the church plant started in the hotel with the golden fish round the ceiling! In many ways it felt like God was bringing a new season of life to the church.

In my personal life my love for spending time with Jesus in the Secret Place was increasing. In my growing hunger to know Him better I found myself developing a new discipline of spending at least fifteen minutes a day just praying in the Spirit in my prayer language; quite often I have found as I do this I receive Holy Spirit revelation on things.

I may be in the autumnal years of my life but it has certainly felt like spring time in my heart as I continually seek to pursue God with all of my heart.

I was really encouraged when not so long ago I was watching Marilyn Hickey powerfully teaching the Word on TV and looking fantastic at eighty two years old. I said to the Lord, 'That's how I want to be until you take me home.' Then I felt God reminding me of the prophecy I had received in Italy years ago – 'The best is yet to come.' I felt Him encouraging me to ignore age and keep pressing in with expectation to the things He reveals to me. I love Psalm 57 verse 2 'I cry out to God Most High, to God, who fulfils His purpose for me.'

I was sharing one day with the Pastor how something I have wrestled with over the years is the lack of understanding as to where my gifting lies within the fivefold ministry gifts. Explaining how I had often thought myself to be a bit of a 'Jack of all trades and Master of none'; I led groups, taught and cared for people, spoke prophetically in to people's lives and led people to the Lord, all of which were covered in the list in Ephesians 4 and then I had the confusion of people saying I had an apostolic ministry. He explained to me how he saw the apostolic ministry as encompassing bits of the other ministries of prophet, pastor, teacher and evangelist. In an instant, the Holy Spirit had switched on a light and I was able to see what others had said to me. My heart always has been and still is, to build up the body of Christ and prepare God's people for works of service. Looking back over the years, I could see how God had used me to build and plant as I encouraged people in their walks with God and had been part of setting up groups that would enable them to grow and flourish.

This also made sense of the mandate that I felt God had given me in recent years to mentor, motivate and mobilise God's people; encouraging them to become more passionate in their love walks with Him serving Him according to the strengths and gifting abilities that He has given them.

I find it quite amazing to look back and see how God has led me through the years in my training to be a reflective practitioner, mentor, family worker – it feels like it was all for such a time as this.

Final Point to Ponder

Would you like to experience the joy that I have found in knowing Jesus?

Then find a quiet place and pray this simple prayer:

> Father God I believe that out of your great love for me you sent Jesus to die on the cross to forgive me for all my wrong-doings.
>
> I am sorry for the things I have done wrong in my life and I receive your forgiveness now. Jesus, I give my life to you and ask you to come in, to be my Saviour and Lord and to take full control of my life from this day on. I ask you to fill me to overflowing with your Holy Spirit. Thank you Jesus, Amen.

Made in the USA
Charleston, SC
19 July 2016